Jane Campion |

Contemporary Film Directors

Edited by James Naremore

The Contemporary Film Directors series provides concise, well-written introductions to directors from around the world and from every level of the film industry. Its chief aims are to broaden our awareness of important artists, to give serious critical attention to their work, and to illustrate the variety and vitality of contemporary cinema. Contributors to the series include an array of internationally respected critics and academics. Each volume contains an incisive critical commentary, an informative interview with the director, and a detailed filmography.

Jane Campion |

Kathleen McHugh

**UNIVERSITY
OF
ILLINOIS
PRESS**
URBANA
AND
CHICAGO

Interviews with Jane Campion by Michel Ciment reprinted
from *Positif* (Jan. 1990), with permission from Michel
Ciment. Interview by Judith Lewis originally published
in *LA Weekly* ("Wholly Jane," Jan. 19, 2000) reprinted by
permission of Judith Lewis. Interview by Lizzie Francke
originally published in *Sight and Sound* ("Dangerous
Liaisons," 13.11: 16–19), reprinted by permission of Lizzie
Francke and *Sight and Sound.*

Library of Congress Cataloging-in-Publication Data
McHugh, Kathleen Anne.
Jane Campion / Kathleen McHugh.
p.   cm. — (Contemporary film directors)
Includes bibliographical references and index.
ISBN-13: 978-0-252-03204-2 (cloth : alk. paper)
ISBN-10: 0-252-03204-7 (cloth : alk. paper)
ISBN-13: 978-0-252-07447-9 (pbk. : alk. paper)
ISBN-10: 0-252-07447-5 (pbk. : alk. paper)
1. Campion, Jane, 1954—Criticism and interpretation.
I. Title.
PN1998.3.C3545M38   2007
791.4302'33092—dc22 [B]   2006036198

Frontispiece: Jane Campion. Photo by Gerald Jenkins.

For Chon |

Contents |

Acknowledgments

This project began with an essay I wrote on Jane Campion published in *Style* early 2001 while at the University of California at Riverside. The insights of my colleagues Piya Chatterjee, Parama Roy, and Carole Anne Tyler enlightened and improved the scope of that essay and their influence remains in this book. In the English department at UCLA, I have enjoyed the support of my department chair, Tom Wortham, and my many colleagues, several of whom offered me valuable suggestions as the book manuscript took shape. Felicity Nussbaum's excellent, detailed feedback on my discussion of Campion's early films greatly strengthened and refined my argument in that section. When it came time to revise my work on Campion's *The Portrait of a Lady*, Jen Fleissner's comments were a godsend; her expertise on James and her astute suggestions helped me to hone and streamline that discussion. Richard Yarborough, who has illuminating and incisive things to say about every film we have ever discussed, has been an inspiration throughout. His observations about Campion's representations of masculinity and race nuanced my overall approach to the book manuscript. I benefit continually from the intellectual companionship provided by Helen Deutsch, Rachel Lee, Harryette Mullen, Jenny Sharp, and Caroline Streeter. Helen has been a wonderful friend on campus and off, providing sage council and fresh ideas on everything from research to fashion.

Outside the department, I owe very special thanks to several mentors and friends. I am grateful for Virginia Wexman's encouragement and her shared passion for Campion. My discussions with Vivian Sobchack, especially regarding *In the Cut*, and her overall feedback on the manuscript were invaluable to me. Barb Klinger rallied my spirits and galvanized my thinking at several crucial junctures in the writing of this book. Her support and that of Jim Naremore have spanned my entire career, and I thank them both for that. I am very grateful to Jim for involving me in this project and for his advice throughout. Thanks also to Joan Catapano and Rebecca Crist from the University of Illinois Press for their help throughout the production process. My writing group—Wendy Belcher, Mary Bush, Ellen Kraut-Hayagawa, Harryette Mullen, and Alice Wexler—read much of the manuscript, sharing their insights over the wonderful dinners we have enjoyed together; I thank them especially for keeping the prose accessible. I would also like to thank the graduate students who assisted me throughout this process: John Bridge; Rebecca Epstein; Kristen Hatch; Jun Okada; Michele Schreiber; and especially Sharon Sharp and Candace Moore, whose labors went far beyond the call of duty. Candace and Brenda Johnson-Grau helped me acquire the cover image, for which I am grateful. Thanks also to neighbor and friend Carla Kaplan for our many walks and talks and to Beth Kalish-Weiss for her resilience, support, and faith in the process.

Jane Campion's work calls us to attend to the mysteries and passions of family, especially among sisters. I would like to thank my sisters, Donna, Jean, and Anne, who have shared these mysteries and passions with me, as well as my brothers, Peter and John, who have participated from a distance. I thank my sister-in-law Betty for her interest in what I do and Julie for her humor and conversation. Thanks to Dick and Robert for their support of my sisters. As the years go by, I discover more and more how much I have in common with my mother; I thank her for our wonderful rush-hour conversations and for starting it all. During the writing of this book, I lost several people who were precious to me: my dear and wonderful colleague, Philip Brett; my brilliant, young, and unfailingly courageous sister-in-law Reni Celeste, who held her mortality at bay far longer than any doctor gave her hope to do; and, lastly, my father, Kenneth McHugh, whose mysteries and passions generated so many of my own.

Finally, I dedicate this book to Chon Noriega, the person with whom I have shared it all.

Jane Campion |

A Vision So Strange and Strong |

Jane Campion became a household name and a filmmaking sensation in 1993 with her third theatrically released feature, *The Piano*. The film won the Palme d'Or at Cannes as well as many other "Best Film" awards that year.[1] Alluding to Andrew Sarris's famous category of outstanding film directors, one critic stated that *The Piano* had catapulted Campion into the "pantheon of great directors" (Margolis 11), yet this award was Campion's second at Cannes. As a graduate student in her second year at the Australian Film Television and Radio School, she had made the film *Peel* (1982), for which she received her first Palme d'Or for "Best Short Film" in 1986. Thus very early in her filmmaking career, Campion garnered the kind of international attention and acclaim that few up-and-coming directors—much less women directors—receive. By mid-career, Campion has made six features; the most recent, *In the Cut*, was released in fall 2003. Although none of her subsequent feature films have generated the same box office or enthusiasm as *The Piano*, Campion continues to explore the controversial and edgy themes that have dominated her work from her first student films up to the present: how power and violence permeate sexual and familial relationships, confound women's self-expression, and reify and distort gender roles. While her perspective on these issues tends to divide and often disturb audiences, one critic observed, after seeing *In the Cut,* "Campion is doing things with sexuality that no one else is."[2] The films that make up her oeuvre explore characters' agency, sexual desire, and drive for self-expression—forces that set them at odds with each other, with the environment, and also, particularly in the case of female characters, with themselves.

At issue in Campion's work are key paradoxes concerning affect and embodiment. Affects and passions are clearly of the body, yet in their throes, one feels, as Judith Butler points out, *"beside oneself,"* dispossessed of one's sense of agency or control (24, emphasis Butler's). In crafting visual stories drawn from genres that are especially attentive to women's bodies, to their agency, their vulnerability, and to their dispossessing passions, Campion generates crises where ethics, vulnerability, sexuality, and violence (or its threat) coalesce. Women are intimately familiar with this terrain, Butler asserts: "Negotiating a sudden and unprecedented vulnerability—what are the options? What are the long-term strategies? Women know this question well, have known it nearly in all times, and nothing about the triumph of colonial powers has made our exposure to this kind of violence any less clear" (42).

Campion's films question the options for the female film protagonist in modes and genres (melodrama, thriller) and situations (dysfunctional families, marriages, relationships) conventionally articulated around her virtue and her suffering. Eschewing that virtue, her films ask, What is the status of the female protagonist's choice, her agency in the context of sexual passions, physical vulnerability, and her own capacity to do harm? How does self-expression emerge from injury and limitation? Bereft of moral resolutions, the political character of these dilemmas and the fact that they are, for the most part, irresolvable in any wholly affirmative or satisfactory sense, emerge forcefully—one possible reason for the intensity and polarization of audiences' responses to Campion's films. One of the aims of this book will be to trace these themes, their timeliness, and their relation to Campion's specific background and historical moment, throughout her work.

To begin, I would like to introduce Jane Campion by combining details from her biography and her self-representation in interviews with contextual information concerning her parents and their position in the arts in New Zealand, her arts and film schooling and their influence on her aesthetic proclivities, and the industry in which she first became a filmmaker. In writing a "thick description" of these contexts, I hope to create a historical basis for understanding her work.

Family

Campion has stated repeatedly that she did not set out to become a filmmaker, though her parents were both prominent figures in New Zealand theater and she grew up in an environment saturated with theater, performance, and film. She was born in Wellington, New Zealand, on April 30, 1954, the second daughter of theater director and producer Richard Campion and writer and actress Edith Campion. Her older sister, Anna, also a film director, was born a year and a half before Jane, and a brother was born seven years after (Cheshire 8–9). Her father, Richard Campion, described by historians as a "giant of New Zealand theater," met Edith Hannah in the mid-1940s around the time that both were featured in George Swan's production of *Winterset*. Early in their marriage, the two traveled to England, where they both worked at the Old Vic Theatre for three years (Harcourt 92–93). Returning in 1951, they embarked on an ambitious undertaking—starting a national professional theater company in New Zealand.

Although many had called for the development of such a company in post–World War II New Zealand, the logistics were daunting. Because the country is composed of two islands, with major population centers distributed throughout rather than clustered together, the geography posed significant challenges. In 1946, critic Russell Reid observed in the Wellington newspaper that "by the very nature of our country, our theater must be a traveling theatre . . . The players would need enthusiasm for the job, courage, and tireless energy" (Harcourt 89). They would also need money, which the Campions had. Edith, orphaned as a child, had inherited a fortune from her grandfather's shoe factory (Cheshire 9), and with her money and the couple's collective talents and commitment, they started the New Zealand Players Company in 1952 and ran it until 1956 (Harcourt 96). The company's principles indicated a commitment to a popular national aesthetic: "To present the best plays of all kinds and, while not pandering to box office appeal, not to present plays [that] cause loss of touch with the audience," and "To find a way of acting, fresh, bold, and sincere, which sprang from and appealed to the people of New Zealand" (Simpson 75). At the same time Richard and Edith were attempting to create this genuine and popular national theater, they were also starting a family. Both Anna and Jane were born during this time and their parents were frequently absent in their pre-school years, writing, directing, acting, traveling with, and running the company. After Campion's brother Michael was born, Edith retired from the theater.

In the early 1960s Richard Campion started the New Zealand Theatre Company, a stationary group located in Wellington (Harcourt 113). He also continued to pursue a distinctive national dramaturgy in his work as a producer, one that incorporated the aesthetics of colonial *pakeha* (New Zealanders of white, European descent) and indigenous Maori cultures. He worked with an all-Maori company that was committed to presenting "indigenous culture" (139–41) and later produced *Green Are the Islands?* an epic about the settling of New Zealand that critics described as unlike anything anyone had ever seen before (145). In it, Campion was keen to represent the difference and conflicts between Maori and European colonial cultures that then culminated in "a rousing finale present[ing] the coming together of all people as New Zealanders" (145).

Interestingly, then, Jane Campion's parents both had a nationally inflected interest in the arts and played a significant role in building an infrastructure for theater production in New Zealand in the 1950s and '60s, as well as contributing to that theater's aesthetics. Further, Jane Campion clearly revisits some of her father's theatrical concerns in her vision of *The Piano*, but does so from a position that refuses a clear national identification with either New Zealand or Australia.[3]

Anthropology, Art, and Early Influences

Coming from this background, Campion initially rebelled when she went to college, wanting nothing to do with theater or acting, interests she had had as a child—"It is loathsome to go and do what your parents did, so I avoided it for a long time" (Wexman, *Interviews,* 6). Instead, she studied anthropology, read Lévi-Strauss, and graduated from Victoria University in Wellington with a bachelor's degree in structural arts in 1975. She later recalled that:

> What interested me about anthropology was to be able to "officially" study what I was curious about anyway: how our thoughts function, their mythic content which has nothing to do with logic, human behaviors. I believe, moreover, that I have an anthropological eye, a sense of observation. I think that humans believe themselves to be rational beings when they are not, they are governed by something completely different. And that's what interests me. But I realized that if I continued in that field I would have to express myself in a way that would only be understood by other anthropologists. (Wexman, *Interviews,* 31)

She left New Zealand for Italy and then England to pursue an education in painting at the Chelsea School of Arts in London. Neither Venice nor London suited her—the former too cold and lonely, the latter too expensive and proper for her forthright manner (155–56). After a year in Europe, she moved to Australia, where she matriculated at the Sydney School of the Arts, graduating in 1979 with a bachelor's degree in painting.

Campion relished her Australian art school experience, mentioning it frequently in interviews and identifying it as a foundational experience in her career: "Art school is where all the learning I did took place" (xii). At the Sydney school, Campion was exposed to the contemporary art world and its global perspective, a perspective that would later clash with the nationalist focus of the film school she subsequently attended. In particular, she has said that Mexican surrealist painter Frida Kahlo (1907–54) and German sculptor Joseph Beuys (1921–86) were particularly formative and important influences on her.[4] Though apparently radically dissimilar, working in different media, countries, periods, and styles, Kahlo and Beuys actually share several qualities that shed light both on Campion's aesthetic development and sensibilities and on the cultural moment in which she did her art training.

Both Kahlo and Beuys came to international prominence while Campion was in art school in the late 1970s. Their fame exemplified the changing character of the world art scene and informed the contemporaneous orientation of the Sydney art school. Beuys was canonized at this time, while Kahlo was "rediscovered." Assessing Beuys's relevance, art historian Robert Hughes observes that while "[t]he sixties produced art world stars with the incontinent frequency of a kid shaking a bag of glitter . . . there were no new art stars in the 1970s except gaunt, moralizing Joseph Beuys in Germany" (365). Art journals of this period deemed Beuys "the greatest living artist of the post-war period" (Ulmer 226), his high art canonization taking place despite the highly political character ("moralizing" to Hughes) of his work; for example, Beuys called for the practice of "Social Sculpture—to mould and shape the world in which we live" and determined that "everyone [is] an artist" (Tisdall 7).

Hughes's view of the art world in the seventies—no new movements, no new stars—pointedly ignores the impact of feminism, civil rights, and third world movements on art in this decade. Among other things, the new focus on women and artists of color resulted in the resurgence of interest in Frida Kahlo, whose work had fallen into obscurity after her death in 1954. In 1978–79, six U.S. museums featured retrospectives of her work, while the Galeria de la Raza in San Francisco held an "Homage to Frida Kahlo" on the Day of the Dead, November 2, 1978. Her biographer, Hayden Herrera, reports that one artist at this event claimed her as a model for "Chicano women" (xii–xiii). Herrera's biography, published in 1983, also added to Kahlo's fame and popularity such that in the late 1970s and early '80s she became "the most popular woman artist in history" (Chadwick 102).

Kahlo and Beuys also share the fact that their vocation as artists was instigated by significant personal traumas and close encounters with death. In each case, the artists subsequently used their own bodies to address, albeit very differently, the materiality of those traumas. Kahlo began painting at nineteen while recovering from a hideous traffic accident that shattered her spine, maimed her right leg and foot, and virtually destroyed her sexual organs and reproductive capacities. Her convalescence immediately after the accident and repeatedly throughout her life (she had thirty-five operations over the twenty-nine years that remained to her) required that she keep still, immobilized in various casts and corsets (Herrera 49, 62). Her paintings, many "wounded self-portraits" (Herrera's term), rendered her body severed, rent open, pierced, and bleeding in surreal and often eroticized images that conveyed yet transformed the materiality of her pain. These works existed in some tension with other of Kahlo's self-portraits, which featured her face imperious, with a fierce, penetrating stare, dressed alternately in indigenous or colonial garb. Interestingly, Laura Mulvey and Peter Wollen, the former who wrote the definitive essay on women as the object of the cinematic gaze in the mid-1970s, asserted that Kahlo, in her self-portraits, made herself the subject rather than object of the gaze:

> [H]er face remains severe and expressionless with an unflinching gaze. At the same time the mask-like face is surrounded by luxuriant growths, accoutrements, ornaments . . . The ornament borders on fetishism, as does all masquerade, but the imaginary look is that of self-regard, therefore a feminine, non-male, and narcissistic look. There is neither coyness or [sic] cruelty, none of the nuance necessary to the male eroticization of the female look. (Quoted in Chadwick 28)

In this context, it is striking and telling that Kahlo was the inspiration for the character of Ada (Holly Hunter) in Campion's film *The Piano* (Wexman 100), and it is understandable how Kahlo informs Campion's innovative approach to female power and sexuality.

Likewise, Beuys work resonates with Campion's "anthropological eyes" as she applies them to violence, trauma, and ritual. Beuys, a Luftwaffe pilot in World War II, was shot down in 1943 on the Russian front and was rescued by Tartar tribesmen who found him unconscious and near death in the snow. "They covered my body in fat to help it regenerate warmth and wrapped it in felt as an insulator to keep the warmth in." As he was unconscious for almost two weeks, "the memories I have of that time are images that penetrated my consciousness" (Beuys in Tisdall, 16–17). After World War II, Beuys experienced debilitating depressions, made art, and became famous in his forties. Declaring that art was "doing or being" rather than "making," he aspired to what he called "'anthropological art,' which could give common human actions the character of ritual" (Hughes 400–403). His sculptures, installations, and "actions" displaced their autobiographical source by literally returning to the material of his experience; he repeatedly explored tactility and envelopment in actions and work that featured fat, felt, blood, dead animals, and beeswax, in quasi-shamanistic healing rituals. Tisdall writes,

"But this does not mean that the fat and felt refer directly to the nomads, or simply to this experience of coming back to life from a state of near death. The state and the properties of the materials remain deeply linked in the mind, and this means that material is imbued with meaning and this meaning can be extended" (17).

Beuys's rituals, both witty and disturbing, drew from "the most subjective, private areas of experience for his handling and treatment of public affairs and objective problems" (Ulmer 229). These qualities and

"Self Portrait with Monkey," surrealist Kahlo's fierce, penetrating stare. Frida Kahlo, 1938, oil on masonite, 16 x 12 in. Reprinted by permission of the Albright-Knox Gallery, Buffalo, New York

Ada's fierce, penetrating gaze in *The Piano* |

the extension of the meaning of materials are evident in *The Pack,* an installation which featured a Volkswagen bus (made by the auto company promoted and funded by Hitler), out of the back of which spill twenty sleds, each equipped with felt, fat, and a flashlight. The piece remotivates everyday objects into something uncanny, suggestive of both threat and survival, healing and horror.

Being "of the moment" in the late seventies, Kahlo and Beuys together indicate the challenges to high modernism being articulated from within its center and from traditions, people, and genres typically excluded from that center. Though much ink will later be spilled concerning Campion's identity as either a New Zealand or Australian filmmaker, such a focus linking the auteur with the nation misses a larger point—the participation of the artist within a global political, social, and aesthetic milieu that includes Mexico and Germany. Furthermore, it seems that a conscious or unconscious symmetry governs her choice of these two figures: a woman exploring the materiality, the surreality of her own pain; a man, the tactility of objects, substances, and rituals of healing. Whereas Kahlo fiercely transformed accident and victimization to vocation and destiny, using her body as medium and instrument, Beuys, a former soldier for the Reich, confronted traumatic guilt and depression and explored their historical materiality and transformation. The German Beuys was internationally celebrated in his own lifetime in the world of "high art." Kahlo's lineage and self-presentation combined colonial, indigenous, and immigrant heritages (her father was a Hungarian Jewish immigrant, her mother of Indian and Spanish descent);

The Pack: Joseph Beuys's anthropological art, 1969. © 2004 Artist Rights Society (ARS), New York/VG Bild-Kunst, Bonn

she became an artist at nineteen and was dead at age forty-eight. The ex-soldier refuses displays of guilt; the violated woman refuses to be a victim. She explores violation and penetration; he, substances and envelopment. Both confound and confirm aspects of gender stereotypes, and together they provide a kind of encryption, or shorthand, for the image Campion begins to construct of herself in the media, and for the aesthetic and thematic concerns that shaped her sensibilities prior to her becoming a filmmaker.

Campion turned from anthropology to art because her interests in mythic thought and in the irrationality that governs human behavior could not find adequate or sufficiently broad means of expression in the former. In art school, she gravitated to artists who rendered experiences of trauma through modes of irrational and mythic expression. Kahlo did so through surrealism, an aesthetic with which Campion has also repeatedly been associated. Because of this admittedly misogynist movement's critique of bourgeois propriety, it provided an inadvertent critique of the institutions (marriage, maternity, and family) that regulated and limited acceptable expressions of femininity. In its focus on the body, its surfaces, and orifices, in its visual evocations of the irrational and its challenge to logical distinctions between inside and outside, conscious and unconscious, self and other, surrealism also provided a ready tool for women artists to explore the female body, femininity, and identity beyond the fundamental cultural binaries that secured an apparently "naturalized" distinction between the genders (Chadwick 4–5). Kahlo "collaps[ed] interior and exterior perceptions of the self" in her self-portraits, a concern that runs through Campion's work (4). Characterizing women surrealists overall, Whitney Chadwick writes that they "display an affinity for structures of fabulist narrative rather than shocking rupture, . . . a tendency towards the phantasmic and oneiric, a preoccupation with psychic powers assigned to the feminine, and an embrace of doubling, masking, and masquerade as defenses against fears of non-identity" (6). Although Campion's films do in certain instances make use of shocking ruptures, they also clearly manifest an interest in the body and its orifices, the use of doubles, masks, and masquerades, and oneiric representations.

If Frida Kahlo's self-portraits make use of surrealism to represent the body, biology, trauma, and the social construction of female identity,

Joseph Beuys invokes the irrational, the mystical, and the shamanistic in his engagements with trauma and healing and the theme of "show your wound." Though not explicitly articulated by Campion as such, her affiliation with Beuys makes itself manifest in several ways: in her obsession with tactility, with objects and the materiality of her mise-en-scène; in the pervasive ambiguities of emotional tone—humor and threat—throughout her work; in her emphasis on the irrational; and finally, in the eccentric kinds of healing and transformation that typically result from the physical traumas that recur in her films.

As mentioned above, Kahlo made such an impact on Campion that she envisioned the Mexican artist as a model for Ada in *The Piano,* insisting that the actress who played her possess Kahlo's look and "power." Campion agreed with an interviewer that the film's narrative also shares aspects of the "tragedy of Frida Kahlo, of her unhappy love life," saying:

> Yes, we have to pay for passions. [W]hen one sees passion as a means of escape, one has to pay dearly for it. I'm fantasizing a little bit. Passion can be the path to happiness as well as to folly. For some people it's like a constant danger area in life, like an addiction. I'm interested in this kind of ultimate experience, which some people need. I feel great sympathy and even adoration for people who attack their lives with such acts of violence. They take a risk and at times they don't survive it." (Wexman, *Interviews,* 100)

What is striking about Campion's "fantasizing" is that she conflates Kahlo and Ada's physical traumas with what she envisions as an element of their own agency, their intense, risk-taking passions—passions that also blend and blur art-making and lovemaking. Though Campion has great respect for their suffering, there is no sense of moralizing Kahlo's or Ada's plight or seeing them as victims; for each, Campion imagines an impassioned, indomitable will.

In her own artwork in school, Campion made what she called "story paintings," her narrative images frequently annotated with dialogue and text. She appreciated the close detailed examination of individual images in art critiques, a practice that allowed her to hone her powers of observation in a creative direction. But she became dissatisfied with the limits of the medium: "I decided I wanted to do work about things I was thinking about and involved in, which were generally relationships and love . . .

and sex! . . . I realized I was trying to storytell, and perhaps I should do the storytelling more directly" (Wexman, *Interviews,* xiii, 52).

Campion thus turned to the medium of film with an extensive background in and a sensibility informed by both ethnography and surrealism, two influences that strongly mark all of her work. As James Clifford points out, the two form a matched set, ethnography setting out to make the strange, the exotic, and the other *familiar,* surrealism endeavoring to make the familiar *strange.* Noting the interconnected onset of both in the early twentieth century, he writes, "The two attitudes presuppose one another; both are elements within a complex process that generates cultural meanings, definitions of self and other. This process—a permanent, ironic play of similarity and difference, the familiar and the strange, the here and the elsewhere—is characteristic of global modernity" (562–63). Significantly, the interrelated attitudes of ethnography and surrealism spring from similarities of method; each depends on unnerving, uncanny, and unexpected juxtapositions (of different cultures or of highly incongruous objects within a given culture) that render cultural experience ironic. "Below (psychologically) and beyond (geographically) any ordinary reality there existed another reality" (Clifford 542). In pursuit of "below" and "beyond" in cinematic storytelling, Campion made her first film, *Tissues,* the following year and, in 1981, she enrolled at the Australian Film Television and Radio School (AFTRS).

Film School, Global Feminism, and Friends

Measured by her output—four films in four years (1981–84), one of which won her the Palme d'Or at Cannes—Campion flourished at AFTRS. In many ways, she was at the right place at the right time and was exactly the right kind of student for AFTRS in the early 1980s. Her perspective on her experience there, however, was very mixed. She found the atmosphere conservative, feeling that the school was just a pipeline for the Australian film industry, and that her instructors didn't get what she was doing or take her seriously (Wexman, *Interviews,* 5, 52). This disparity between Campion's experience and its outcome can be understood in a larger context having to do with the orientation of AFTRS, the coordinates of national cinemas and their relation to art cinema, and finally the Australian film industry in the early 1980s, which was particularly geared to promoting women filmmakers.

AFTRS developed from a set of nationalist priorities at odds with the transnational perspective of the world art scene that shaped Campion's experience at the Sydney School of the Arts. The idea for a national film school was proposed in the early 1960s as "part of the Commonwealth Government's strategy to promote the development of Australia's Cultural Activity." Its plan drew from the model of other national film schools in the face of resistance from people within the Australian film industry, who advocated the creation of a trade school with an apprentice program rather than "an arty-farty institution." The derision evident in the industry responses (and AFTRS's advertising of these responses on their Web site) speaks to the schizophrenic demands on and identities of many national film industries in the post-WWII era.

The postwar reorganization and decline of the Hollywood studio system, due to legal challenges and the rise of TV (among other factors), lowered the U.S. industry's film output. The consequent need for product, together with European interests in state funding and promotion of their national cinemas, allowed for resurgence of these cinemas on the international market. Financially, these national cinemas needed commercial success internationally to survive, and they competed successfully with Hollywood primarily as aestheticized alternatives to Hollywood's mass culture norms. This alternative, consolidated as a discreet film practice known as "art cinema," prioritizes realism ("real problems," "real locations," and explicit "realistic" sexuality) and directorial expressivity, the latter marked by stylistic deviations from Hollywood cinema (Bordwell, "The Art Cinema," 716). In this way, the postwar construction of various national cinemas has been intimately connected with auteurism, the "director as great artist" theory of cinematic production. Consequently, the goal of national industries and national films schools was to produce filmmakers whose vision would be sufficiently distinct from the Hollywood model to be claimed for a uniquely national perspective, while also remaining sufficiently similar to that model to be commercially viable in the international film market. The Australian industry's resentment at the formation of AFTRS, but, even more notably, AFTRS's interest in promoting their identity as an "arty" institution, derives from this pressure for an aestheticized type of production that is nevertheless commercial (and therefore relies on but does not acknowledge stock in trade skills).

In 1972, Minister Peter Howson officially announced the formation of the Australian Film Television School (radio was added to the name and the curriculum in 1981); it admitted its first twelve students the following year, among whom were Gillian Armstrong, Phillip Noyce, and Chris Noonan. The school's first head, Jerzy Toeplitz, gestured at the nationalist aesthetics informing its mission when he asserted that the school's concerns went beyond practical, technical filmmaking skills, and included the development of "the intelligence and imagination of film makers" (AFTRS Web site). Thus Campion's technical training took place in an institution nominally committed to an art, rather than a trade, orientation to the cinema.

Practically, this mission dictated required units in screen studies to supplement the production courses in the various degree programs. Screen studies included courses in film and television genres, national cinemas, auteurs ("Great Filmmakers and Their Films"), and film adaptation as well as courses on the Australian industry and Australian screen culture (AFTRS Web site). These courses neatly blend commercial and nationalist orientations (film and television genres, Australian industry, Australian screen culture) with the individualist aesthetics of art cinema (national cinemas, auteurs, film adaptation). In so doing, the screen studies curriculum was tailored to prepare its students for the challenges facing Australian cinema and its filmmakers in this period. Robson and Zalcock write, "It is not unusual to find the films of the New Australian Cinema adopting the generic conventions of commercial Hollywood movies. Australia's national cinema had to address the twin demands of a 'quality' cinema that would deal with specifically Australian themes and the commercial requirement that the films do well internationally. As a result, the films of this period are balanced between 'art-house' and commercial—a familiar dilemma for many national cinemas" (11).

It was that part of AFTRS's mission directed to enhancing the national industry and its commercial success that troubled Campion and clashed with her art school background. She entered film school with the intention to find "her own voice," rather than a place in the Australian film industry (Wexman, *Interviews*, 52). Ironically, it was precisely that individualist, aesthetic background that made her ideally suited for both AFTRS and the Australian national film industry. In her own interests, she embodied the "familiar dilemma" facing the Australian national cinema at that time. Her filmmaking therefore emerges from a conscious and self-conscious awareness of auteurism and art cinema, as well as of the generic and stylistic conventions of industry cinema, two approaches whose diverse priorities have both enabled and sometimes impeded her success.

Campion also fortuitously came of age in an era and national industry transformed by feminism. The planning and formation of AFTRS was the first part of a broadly based government initiative in the 1970s and early '80s to foster national film production through state funding for filmmakers, tax concessions for private investment in the industry, and the creation of national awards and festivals to showcase New Australian cinema (Robson and Zalcock 2). This initiative resembled the similarly state-supported resurgence of European national/auteurist cinemas in the 1950s and '60s. Yet in Australia in the 1970s and '80s, the government initiative was influenced by global feminism, and the revival of the industry in the 1970s therefore either directly involved or coincided with the creation of the Women's Film Fund (administered by the Australian Film Commission), the Sydney Women's Film Group, the Women's Programme, and other organizations that provided funding, workshops and training, and distribution and exhibition for women's films (Robson and Zalcock 3, Stern 314). Among the luminaries of this cinema's first generation (Peter Weir, Bruce Beresford) was Gillian Armstrong, of the first cohort at AFTRS and the director of *My Brilliant Career* (1979).[5] Campion's class at AFTRS included other art school students turned filmmakers—Sally Bongers and Su Brooks (a career path also followed by Alison MacLean, Gaylene Preston, and Alexis Hunter) (Robson and Zalcock 32). Thus, the confluence of arts training, AFTRS, and feminism launched the careers of many of the women soon to dominate the Australian and New Zealand film industries. Campion entered both the film school and the Australian film industry in what was the beginning of the most auspicious moment for women in that industry's history.[6]

Whatever Campion's problems with AFTRS's ideologies, she did appreciate the financial and technical support she received there: AFTRS funded her first four films and supplied the necessary equipment for them (Cheshire 18–19). Perhaps the greatest resources afforded by the school, however, were the artistic collaborators she met either in or through the school, many of whom were women. On her first film, *Mishaps: Seduction and Conquest* (1981) (later released as *Mishaps of Seduction and Conquest*), the crew consisted of twice as many women as men. One of the four camera operators on that film was Sally Bongers. Bongers and Campion hit it off immediately, and Bongers went on to do the cinematography on three of Campion's subsequent, prize-winning films: *Peel* (1982) and *A Girl's Own Story* (1984), both made at AFTRS, and *Sweetie* (1989), Campion's first theatrically released feature. All three possess a distinctive visual style that has been attributed to Bongers's sensibility. Whereas *Peel*, Campion's second student film, is an experimental primer featuring many diverse techniques of editing and cinematography, *A Girl's Own Story* and *Sweetie* both exhibit a coherent sense of Bongers's style, characterized by the use of wide-angle lenses, eccentric low- and high-angle and tight, claustrophobic framings, and quirky and highly noticeable uses of mobile framing.[7] Campion also met novelist Gerald Lee at AFTRS (writer, producer, and, for awhile, boyfriend) who cowrote and codirected *Passionless Moments* and who cowrote *Sweetie*. Finally, Veronika Haeussler began working with Campion as editor on *Passionless Moments* and served in that capacity on all her subsequent features except for her made-for-TV feature, *Two Friends*.

The Early Films

Jane Campion entered the Australian Film Television and Radio School in 1981 and graduated in 1984. During her time there, she made four short films: *Mishaps: Seduction and Conquest* (1981); *Peel: An Exercise in Discipline* (1982); *Passionless Moments* (1983); and *A Girl's Own Story* (1984). Though the bulk of critical analysis on her work understandably focuses on her feature films, these early shorts provide a crucial template for her later, more well-known work. Despite the endless critiques of auteur theory, some of which have explicitly cited the example of Jane Campion, this director's films demonstrate a remarkable if complex consistency of narrative, thematic, and stylistic concerns that run from her student films up to her most recently released feature, 2003's *In the Cut*.[8] The early shorts, edgy and explicit, focus on power, violence, and emotional pain in dysfunctional sexual, familial, and social relationships. Campion has said, "As a very young filmmaker I was particularly committed to what was nasty, what isn't spoken about in life" (Wexman, *Interviews*, 9). She was also committed to stylistic experimentation, readily evidenced in the innovative techniques and visual quality of these early works. But she was not gratuitously so. To complicate her audiences' perspective on the taboo subjects she addressed, Campion employs cinematic techniques that both represent and blur the differences between objective and subjective narrative states. Dramatically synthesizing documentary or ethnographic with subjective, often surreal cinematic modes, the films convey a sense of astute psychological realism shot through with an ironic, perverse, and highly visual wit.

In her student films and her later features, children, men, and their suffering share focus with and are integral to Campion's representations of femininity. In fact, Jane Campion has never made a film exclusively about heterosexual romance. Rather, such relationships are always represented in the context of, and often dwarfed in importance by, relationships between siblings, parents and children, and friends. The men in her films are frequently inadequate and diffident, but Campion also does not shy away from depicting the ways that women's passions and impulsive behavior bring disaster on themselves. And though children are frequently hapless pawns in adult relationships, Campion depicts them as possessed of cunning, rages, and passions as intense as or more so than any adult.[9] Finally, in her first student film, Campion explores a theme to which she returns again and again, one that tends to subsume romance and emotion as priorities in her features: the importance of women's work, their creative expression, and of sexual desire as a powerful, necessary, and compelling *threat* to that expression. That Campion won her first Palme d'Or for one of her student films is not at all surprising—they evidence, in compressed form, the visual and thematic sophistication and concerns that later drew the attention of the international film community with her release of *The Piano* twelve years after she made her first student film in 1981.

Seduction and Conquest

For her first project at AFTRS, Campion chose to represent the "two different styles of conquest." Reading accounts of famed British climber

George Mallory's failed 1924 attempt to summit Mount Everest, Campion was intrigued by the mountaineers' descriptions of the peak as "a temptress: the closer you got to it the less you wanted it . . . just like the nature of desire" (Wexman, *Interviews,* 5). She invented a fictional brother for George named Geoffrey, whose conquest was the attempted seduction of a writer named Emma, and the film implicitly aligns the two brothers' respective goals: the distant, unapproachable mountain peak and the aloof professional woman. Campion wrote, directed, and edited the video, originally titled *Mishaps: Seduction and Conquest* (1981). The narrative opens with a scroll that reads, "In 1924 a British Party of climbers made a second attempt to conquer Mount Everest. It ended in tragedy. Amongst the climbers was George Mallory. Here we record his letters to his brother Geoffrey and Geoffrey's replies . . .".[10]

Though the text might lead us to expect an opening of one of the brothers writing or reading a letter, the visuals present us with what seems to be a classic scene of voyeurism. First we see a hallway at the end of which a man stands in front of a door. Glancing surreptitiously down the hall (in the direction of the camera) to ensure he is not being watched, the man then bends over and looks through the keyhole. The next shot, in which we share his point of view through the keyhole, shows us the object of his attention: a woman writing and reading busily at her desk. As the camera cuts back to its original position, we see the man straighten up, walk toward the camera, and sit dejectedly on a heater in the foreground of the shot.

A voiceover intones "Dear Mallory," as we cut to grainy brown newsreel footage of base camp on Mount Everest, 1924. We see the climbers standing in front of tents and at a table eating, then a still of the whole party over which the camera passes, coming to rest on the doomed figure of George Mallory. Throughout we hear Geoffrey's letter to his brother:

> Dear Mallory—At last: a woman who is not always batting eyelashes and planning tea parties. She's a writer and has a column in a journal. I fear I am a little in love. She however seems quite indifferent, only noticing me should an errand arise . . . I trust only that my visits remain unnoticed and Elizabeth unsuspicious. It is marvelous to know that as you glance up from my letter you may well be in sight of Everest. Do take care. Don't lose any toes. Your loving and admiring brother, Geoffrey.

Geoffrey as voyeur in *Mishaps: Seduction and Conquest*

Geoffrey's object of desire in *Mishaps*

At the close of the letter, the scene shifts back to writer Emma's room, comprising a sleeping area in the background on the left, a desk in the foreground of the shot, and a sitting area on the right. Emma sits at her desk, facing the camera, writing busily, hardly looking up as she rebuffs Geoffrey's invitations to tea and to any conversation.

After looking longingly at and hovering around her, Geoffrey finally retreats to the side of the room and reads his brother's response to him. George recounts his first glimpse of his goal: "The clouds parted to afford my first view of Everest. I was not disappointed. This was a true peak, thrusting up sharply into the sky, a silver trail billowing out to the east like a bridal veil. My step faltered, my own stature seemed shrunken, but my will was secured. I would climb Everest." George's look at Everest produces a contradictory description and ambivalent response. He describes Everest in terms both phallic—"thrusting up sharply"—and feminine—"its silver, billowing bridal veil." The view humbles him—he stumbles and feels shrunken—but it also precipitates his resolve—he will climb Everest. In his final communications to his brother, he notes that the closer he gets to the peak, the more "the altitude strips us of desire." His final meditation has to do with his will and his goal, both seemingly distinct from his desire: the severity of Everest is "so murderous that if you had any sense, you would do well to hesitate on the threshold of the ultimate goal and tremble."

As these opening sequences make clear, brothers George and Geoffrey, as well as writer Emma, are all obsessed with different objects of desire. Yet, in a clever turn of gender conventions, for most of the piece, we only have access, through the letters, to *George* and *Geoffrey's* subjectivities, to their desires and thoughts about their goals. We simply see Emma write, worry about deadlines, and refuse distractions; she is preoccupied, inaccessible to Geoffrey and to us. George and Geoffrey's different "styles" of conquest are starkly contrasted by the crosscutting between contemporary black-and-white footage depicting Geoffrey's attempted seduction of Emma, and newsreel footage documenting George Mallory's Everest expedition. The wit and audacity of this montage is oddly both ameliorated and enhanced by the letters between the two brothers that bring the film's real and fictional worlds into plausible correspondence.

Campion achieves several meanings through this sound and image montage. First, she aligns the two styles of conquest with two styles of suffering, one emotional, the other physical: Geoffrey plays errand boy and endures Emma's cold and humiliating indifference in his attempted conquest of her, just as his brother George submits to frostbite, to paralyzing fatigue, and, finally, to death in his pursuit of Everest's peak. In a motif that will recur throughout Campion's work, here desire burns, moves one forward, but also freezes, literally or figuratively arresting one's movement altogether. Second, the elaborate montage of the piece, which Campion herself referred to as "more sophisticated than some of my other stuff" (Wexman, *Interviews*, 5), aligns a world historical moment of (failed) conquest—George Mallory's tragic 1924 Everest expedition—with a fictional personal seduction, Geoffrey's conquest of a woman writer who is visually compared with Everest at the film's conclusion. While the irony generated by this comparison is formidable, the film also exploits the cross-contamination of public and private conquests its montage affords. That is, if the comparison makes Geoffrey appear a bit ridiculous, the erotic impulses underlying George's quest are also strongly underscored. Along these same lines, Campion compares Geoffrey's voyeurism, his longing looks at the impervious and preoccupied Emma, with George's glimpse of Everest and his resolve to conquer the peak. Each of the brother's endeavors involve vision, the contemplation of the object of desire, and the effects of that vision on the would-be conqueror.

The video's visuals reiterate the conceit of the narrative, incorporating documentary footage, grainy, brown, and ravaged, of Mallory's historical adventure with fictional diegetic footage of brother Geoffrey. Clearly the video contrasts at every level, from quality of the film stock to the content of the images to the two narratives themselves, the two styles of conquest. What are those styles? For George, the very immensity of his goal, the impossibility of attaining it, both weakens his stature and his desire, while it resolves his will. Though he rationally understands that he should hesitate and tremble in the face of this will, he nevertheless presses on and dies. Geoffrey compares his conquest to that of his brother, using language very much like George's: "My will is set and I cannot remove myself without being told to go. Perhaps the penalties are not as severe as Everest, but I am stuck on a small ledge and cannot find a foothold." Yet unlike his brother, Geoffrey, depressed by Emma's continuing indifference, gives up. He stays away, telling her, "I won't be visiting so often so you won't be bothered by me." As a result of his submission and abjection, as well as his performance of a "manly" task of fixing her light bulb, Emma misses him, warms to him, and they become intimate.

The consequence of Geoffrey's submission, his giving up, is that Emma gives in. As if mimetically infected with Geoffrey's abject desire, she kisses him aggressively, giving him what he then finds he no longer wants. They switch positions. Geoffrey leaves, telling Emma he is not certain when he will be back. The film's finale? Emma sits at her desk, fussing with Geoffrey's scarf, wrapped tellingly around her neck. She picks up her pen and freezes—she cannot write. Frustrated, she throws it down and the film ends. In a certain sense, this is a very old story. Freud wrote about it, about men and women being a phase apart. But in the context of Campion's subsequent feature films, which all have to do with female self-expression in some form or another, it bears a closer look.

Interestingly, though the majority of this film is about two brothers, their confidences to each other, and their relative styles of seduction and conquest, it ends with a dramatic shift, suddenly about a woman writer's loss of focus and ability to write after she has been seduced and politely abandoned. Geoffrey's seduction, his (should we call it success-ful?) conquest of Emma bears a striking resemblance to the narrative of *The Piano* in which Baines's (Harvey Keitel) final and successful move in his barter/seduction of Ada is that he gives up, telling her he is wretched from wanting her. He gives her piano back to her, a piano that she is then little interested in playing.[11] In each case, the woman, engaged in her own art, her own endeavors, becomes infected by the failed desire of the other, and then loses herself to that position. This narrative trope, of the man and woman switching places, gaining and losing power, first impervious, then suffering and vice versa, signals a tendency that Campion will later explore repeatedly in her subsequent work. Her scripts frequently feature characters across genders, genera-tions, and cultures who imitate, impersonate, and switch roles with each other as their positions of power, their desires, and the narrative's focus radically shift as well.

In *Mishaps*, Campion subtly prepares for this shift by using the character of Emma to complicate the neat parallel her film ostensibly establishes between the "two styles" of conquest. Early on, the film makes a tacit comparison between Emma and George when we hear Geoffrey's first letter describing her as "not always planning tea parties . . . she's a writer." As he stresses her independence, her uniqueness among women, we see footage of Mallory and his expedition at base camp. Their monumental struggle to climb Everest in 1924 is compared to Emma's independence and career as a writer during the same period. In the comparison the film makes between "public" or world historical conquest, which commands documentation in newsreels, newspapers, and history books, and "private" romantic conquest, which dominates imaginative prose and film fiction, Emma's character suggestively bridges both—she is a journalist and she bears the name of one of Jane Austen's most famous novels and protagonists. Similarly, Emma does not fall neatly within either "style" of conquest; like George, she is engaged in her own monumental conquest (as an independent woman supporting herself by her writing) and like Everest, she is the object of Geoffrey's conquest. It is only when she responds to him, attempts to take his place as a desiring subject, that she fails.

Finally, though only a subtext, colonialism is a concern in *Mishaps*, one which will also recur in Campion's later works. Mount Everest, sitting on the border between Tibet and Nepal, has been historically appropriated by Britain, as we can assume that the Tibetans and Nepalese did not know the peak by the name of Everest. Indeed, after World War I, the British were "obsessed" with conquering the highest mountain in the world. Writing of the initiative that led to Mallory's expedition, Peter Firstbrook observes, "Both the north and south poles had been 'conquered' before the war, on both occasions by 'foreigners.' National prestige was now at stake and the consensus at the Royal Geographic Society was that this last great objective, the 'Third Pole' should be a British triumph" (2). Ironically neither of the first two climbers to reach the summit in 1953 were British, though they made the ascent under the British flag—Sir Edmund Hillary was Campion's compatriot from New Zealand, and Tenzing Norgay was Nepalese. In choosing the British Mallory's earlier expedition, Campion was clearly interested in the climbers' obsession and failure, both of which sprang from nationalist and colonialist impulses. Mallory might also have appealed as an eccentric, upper-middle-class figure who was a darling of the Bloomsbury group

(James Strachey was his classmate at Cambridge, Duncan Grant painted him nude, and the others made much of his physical beauty), a staunch leftist, and an early and strong supporter of women's rights (Anker and Roberts 43–44, 51).[12] In aligning his 1920s endeavor with his brother's conquest of an obviously independent woman, the film implicates, at least historically, white European women's emancipation with British imperialism, a motif explored in *The Piano,* and, in the milieu of the postcolonial, in *Holy Smoke* as well.

In *Mishaps,* certain techniques and proclivities of Campion's film-making are already clearly present, most notably the use of voiceover and the blend of tragedy and self-reflexive cinematic humor. All of Campion's feature films make use of voiceover narration, a feature of her work that I will discuss throughout. Her films also easily mix tragic, even horrific, events with aesthetic and thematic perspectives and concerns that are wittily evoked. The opening shot where Geoffrey glances directly at the camera to make sure he is not being watched typifies the latter. A parody of industry cinema's insistent positioning of women as objects of the gaze, the camera's set-up (in both senses of the term) both mimics and inverts the gender positions of this industry convention. Here we watch the voyeur, who is presented as both petulant and abject. We then take up his gaze as he secretly looks not on the object of his desire undressing or naked or bathing, but writing and working. In a lovely visual rewriting of John Berger's famous assertion that women watch themselves being watched (46), the voyeur, in looking at the camera, watches us watching him, before we then take up his point of view. This complex joke ironizes the visual field, splitting its address to the spectator in two. Within the sense of the narrative, we watch the voyeur make sure he is not being watched; within the framing of the shot, we receive his gaze as the sly joke of the filmmaker, an extra-narrative aside that aligns us with her perspective and the visual double entendre of this scene.

In its final sequence, *Mishaps* transforms the overt parallel that has structured it up to this point. Geoffrey conquers Emma by eliciting her desire, by making himself the object of her erotic conquest. Emma then lays down her pen, her failure aligning her with George Mallory. He died on Everest, she can no longer write; yet the business of the film goes beyond our identification with these characters. It suggests through the wit and audaciousness of its montage that we contemplate the ironies, across genders, of work, will, desire, suffering, conquest, and seduction and their inextricable relation to one another—whether one's object is a mountain, a woman, or aesthetic expression.

Discipline

If Campion's first student film self-reflexively engages the parallels between two different orders of connection—montage and erotics—her second, *Peel: An Exercise in Discipline* (1982), uses a virtuosity of technique to deconstruct several types of discipline. Campion edited, wrote, and directed *Peel*, while Sally Bongers did the cinematography on this, Campion's first and only student film in color. Peopled again by siblings in a triad of characters, two male (redheads) and one female (auburn), the film replaces the erotic relation with an emphasis on generations. It depicts the heated conflicts that arise on a car trip taken by a working or lower-middle-class Australian family, playing themselves, comprised of Tim Pye and his sister Katie, both in their late twenties or early thirties, and Tim's seven-year-old son, Ben. As perhaps suggested by their red hair, this family is volatile and hot-headed. Katie is upset with her brother Tim because he is ignoring her opinion about a piece of property they have just looked at and she wants to get home to her soap opera. Clearly not involved in the conversation, nor in the business of the car trip, little Ben is bored. He tosses an orange against the windshield to pass the time, then peels it and throws the peels out the window, despite his father's increasingly more vehement injunctions that he not do so. Tim pulls over, slams on the brakes, and orders Ben to go pick up all the peels. Katie is furious that the delay will cause her to miss her TV show. While Tim goes to find Ben, she peels another orange and drops the peels on the ground. When they return, Tim and Ben order her to pick them up. She refuses. They sit, traffic goes by, Ben jumps on the roof of the car. The film ends.

Yet again, the business of *Peel* exceeds the dilemmas of its characters, as is signaled by its subtitle, rendered in orange type in the film's opening frame: "An Exercise in Discipline." Eight shots follow in quick succession, which alternate between orange text and traffic signs and images. A very quick shot of blue and white traffic arrows whizzing by is followed by the film's title, *Peel*, then cars whizzing by, then a list of the cast (Tim Pye, Katie Pye, Ben Martin), then traffic arrows, then a triangle patterned on a Lévi-Strauss kinship schematic, reiterating the actors' names and their relation to one another:

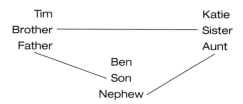

One more shot of whizzing cars and then the statement: "A TRUE STORY/A TRUE FAMILY."

A coy parody of industry films that simultaneously solicit heightened spectatorial seriousness and voyeurism in their telling of "a true story," this opening complements that of *Mishaps,* each film referencing one of the two voyeurisms that interest Campion—erotic and realist. This statement also suggests that Campion and crew made this film to fulfill the first year directing students' assignment to make a short documentary on a subject of the student's choice. As reviewers and critics have observed, the film that follows certainly qualifies as a student exercise in the discipline of filmmaking, displaying considerable skill and flourish in its highly noticeable uses of editing, cinematography, sound, and mise-en-scène (Paskin 211, Polan 64). Yet the film cleverly foils its twin exercises to tell a true story and to exhibit technical acumen in the telling by pitting the two against each other. That is, the virtuosity of the filmmaking, by drawing attention to itself, exceeds its function of invisibly conveying or documenting the "true" story that it tells. In the opening sequence, for example, the striking alternation between static shots of orange text and rapid mobile shots of blue and white traffic signs is appointed by a rhythmic pulse on the soundtrack—bam, bam, bam—the source of which we only belatedly discover is Ben's bouncing the orange on the dashboard of the car. In addition, what we hear is not faithful to its source, the sound much more like a tennis or basketball being bounced than an orange. In the lack of sound fidelity, the act of representation is foregrounded. In other words, how Campion is telling this "true" story, the film's form, is as noticeable and interesting as the story itself.

Paskin and Polan have also noted that this formal exercise is matched by a narrative concerned with parental discipline as Tim attempts (and fails) to teach his son a lesson about obedience. Actually the film depicts instances of failed discipline among all its characters, carefully delineating how these failures relate to hierarchies of kinship (Bloustien 1). In so doing, Campion exercises the rhetoric of another discipline in which she had training; she clearly references anthropology in the film's use of the kinship schematic and the text, "A TRUE FAMILY." *Peel* enacts a mock ethnography of this "true family," using cinematic technique to transform abstract concepts and schematic kinship principles into its visual and narrative logic.

How does this proceed? Following the film's opening montage, we get a sequence of shots within the constricted space of a moving car. Campion and Bongers triangulate the small, cramped area, moving within it as if they were moving around the kinship triangle with which the film opens. They begin at its base, the apex formed by the younger and therefore less powerful generation. We see Ben as he bounces an orange off the windshield, these visuals finally matching the amplified and slightly distorted sound of a ball bouncing that is audible from the beginning of the film. Shot from the side at a low angle, we see only his side, his arms, his legs, as we hear his aunt sharply criticizing the "scrappy piece of land" they have just looked at. The next shot, of Katie, captures only her face and shoulders from a frontal perspective; she is sitting in shadow behind her brother in the back seat and loudly complains, "If you don't want other opinions, don't ask for them." As she talks, the camera shifts to Tim, depicting only the back of his seat and his head. He signals his displeasure by not responding.

These three opening shots exercise three possible visual perspectives—side, front, and back—as they also stage the first axis of conflict, here aural, between Katie and Tim. The subsequent film will systematically chart its conflicts along each axis of familial connection. Instead of reciprocating Katie's anger at him, Tim gets angry at Ben, yelling at him not to throw any more peels out the window. As Ben argues with and disobeys his father, the editing and perspective focuses on them and alternates between the inside and the outside of the car. We get our first view of Tim's face in close-up as he shouts at his son. We hear Katie trying to intervene in the escalating conflict by offering Ben a piece of cake and we see his face for the first time when he turns around for a dramatic close-up, yelling, "No!" His aunt pulls his hair, Ben shakes the now peeled orange in front of his father's face, and then in quick succession, we get a shot of Tim's foot hitting the brakes, Katie's hand gripping a leather armrest, and then Ben slamming forward and back in his seat. Tim leans over, opens Ben's door, yelling, "Get out!" He tells him to get out and go pick up every single peel he's thrown out. A series of shots then depicts Ben outside the car, Tim and Katie inside, arguing about getting home in time.

In rapid order, we have moved from Katie versus Tim, to Tim versus Ben, to Ben versus Katie, to Tim versus Ben again, and then back to Katie versus Tim. Adult siblings Katie and Tim, in a lateral rather than hierarchical relation to each other, clash, their conflict expressed by her verbal remonstrations and his silence. Because they are equals and neither can really discipline the other, their squabbles reduce them both to children. Ben, caught between them, serves as an intermediary for their rage. As in many Campion narratives, inadequately disciplined adults treat children as peers, conduits, and translators, siphoning off erotic and aggressive energy through them. Frequently these adults are a heterosexual couple or in an erotic triangle or they are siblings. These adult conflicts foster intergenerational ones, as Ben refuses first his father's, then his aunt's authority to discipline him.

When Tim gets out of the car to make Ben go pick up the peels, the filmmaker exploits the possibilities of open space, even as the axis of conflict continues to move around the triangle of relations. Lateral tracking shots, rhythmic editing, foreground/background relations, crosscutting, uses of contrasts and parallels in right-left, left-right screen direction are all exercised as Ben disappears, Katie stomps off and urinates in the bushes, and Tim goes to find Ben. Campion has a particular fondness for depicting women urinating outdoors (*Sweetie, The Piano, Holy Smoke*), a motif of a piece with her insistence on showing or referring to bodies, their orifices, and excretions. Katie's outdoor urination grants this "true story" a kind of bodily or physical credibility to match its depiction of family dysfunction.

The film's finale comes as Ben and Tim, who have been reconciled (Tim is greatly impressed that Ben has successfully reassembled most of the orange peel), make their way back to the car. Ben is on Tim's shoulders, and shots of Tim doing different kinds of steps, to Ben's great amusement, alternate with shots of Katie's orange peels, dropping thump, thump (reminiscent of the bouncing sound at the beginning of the film) on the ground, the thumps keeping time with Tim's steps. Finding Katie's pile of peels, Tim demands that she pick them up. She ignores him. In a gendered solidarity, Ben mimics his father in both phrase and intonation, yelling at her to pick them up. Katie ignores him as well. The film falls silent, save for the whoosh of passing cars. Successive close-ups of all three characters' faces, who share freckles and coloring, are ultimately grafted together—Katie's eyes, Tim's nose, Ben's chin. In the final shot sequence, two medium shots depict Katie sitting in the front seat, Tim on the back bumper. Three final shots, from the perspective of three cars traveling by the Pye's parked car at high speed (first screen right to screen left, then left to right, then right to left again) show Ben jumping on the roof of the car, the rhythm of his impact again mimicking the sound of the orange that opens the film. The kinship triangle charting family and power relations has been fully materialized and inverted through its systematic exploration by the film. Now Katie and Tim's lateral relation forms the base of the triangle, while above and between them, Ben bounces on the roof.

Peel's "true story" contains truly disturbing representations of breakdowns in adult behavior and relentless family conflict, punctuated by moments of real or threatened violence. Tim sends his son off to pick up every piece of the orange peel on the side of the road despite the cars driving along it at rapid speeds. Ben does what he is told, and charms his father and us, as we see him kneeling, bent over in the dirt, the fully reconstructed orange peel a globe cupped in his hands. As cars whiz by a few feet away from him, the humor and horror of the moment coalesce. The film also possesses a highly self-conscious formal structure and distanced perspective that simultaneously performs and mocks the viability of disciplinary exercises, especially those directed to producing "truth." The relation of the film's subtitle, which comes first, to its title seems to encompass the larger problematic on which this film is an extended meditation. The pun of the film's title, peel, signifies both an object and an action. At cross or paradoxical purposes to one another, peel is both what covers, hides, protects, and the act of cutting away or removing that cover or protection. Similarly, a peel is both the whole and any part separated from it. These multiple meanings, visualized and enacted here with an orange, provide a material analogue for the much more abstract, but no less paradoxical relation proposed by the necessity of making a film which is "an exercise in discipline." *Peel's* exercise in discipline produces an object, the film *Peel*, whose paradoxical status is both that of an action, an approximation (an exercise), and an object, the real thing ("a true story").

As suggested by its opening sequence, wherein static text and diagram alternate with rapidly moving images, *Peel* sets about materializing the conundrum of noun versus verb and object versus action by converting the abstraction of language and diagram into images, bodies, action, and the multiple perspectives afforded by film techniques. As with *Mishaps*, *Peel* demonstrates the filmmaker's ongoing and focused exploration of the relationship between spoken or written words and moving images, evident both in her consistent output of film adaptations (half of her theatrically released features are adaptations: *An Angel at My Table*, *Portrait of a Lady*, and *In the Cut*) and in the language play that runs throughout all her work. In this film, Campion explicitly investigates the means whereby abstract signs, directions, and diagrams

Ben reassembles the orange peel in *Peel* |

can be transformed into concrete images and narratives. A schematic of names, roles, and kinship relations becomes characters, relationships, conflicts, and the spatial template for shot configurations. The double meaning of an "exercise in discipline" becomes concretized in the action and object denoted by the film's title, *Peel*. Here Campion makes a short film, documenting how moving images can apprehend abstractions; she borrows concepts and schematic from one discipline, anthropology, to structure the disciplinary procedures of another, nonfiction filmmaking, and in the process, illuminates and deconstructs both.

Moments

Whereas *Peel* focuses on film technique, dialogue, and character conflict, Campion's third student film, *Passionless Moments* (1983)—codirected and written with Gerald Lee—renders an ethereal ethnoscape of a Sydney neighborhood. Like *Mishaps*, this film blends claims to an objective documentary realism and immediacy, albeit inflected with surreal visual flourishes, and a relentless focus on character interiority and all manner of subjective states and processes. The film is comprised of ten anecdotal fragments or vignettes, seven devoted to men or boys, three to a middle-aged woman, a teenager, and a girl, respectively. The film's full title, *Passionless Moments: Recorded in Sydney Australia Sunday October 2*, suggests an interest in immediate circumscribed increments of time ("Moments"), precisely identified and documented ("Recorded in Sydney Australia Sunday October 2"), yet coyly avoids becoming "dated" by not listing a year. Yet the film takes on these objective parameters only to turn its attention to subjective states outside the operations of narrative sequence and causality. All of the film's otherwise disparate vignettes explore the capacity of the cinema to represent internal psychological states. They do so through a sophisticated and sustained use of voiceover narration in conjunction with an emphasis on filmic sound honed and focused by a complete absence of dialogue. Each vignette runs from forty-five seconds to a minute and a half long, and each has an enigmatic and frequently humorous title, subsequently revealed as taken directly or paraphrased from the omniscient male voiceover narration that explicates it.

Generally eschewing conventions of cinematic meaning predicated on sequence—narrative causality or any sexualized or "passionate" interaction that progresses (the gay couple in the vignette "Focal Lengths" aren't speaking or doing anything else)—Campion and Lee instead focus on strategies to condense and compress meaning within the limited framework of each moment: visual and verbal puns, allegory, allusions of all sorts, cinematic self-reflexivity. In patterning the voiceover and the images in variable relations to one another—explanatory, redundant, ironic, and enigmatic—the filmmakers also investigate the representational possibilities made available by the film's absence of dialogue. But most important to Campion's later films is *Passionless Moments'* sustained interest in the cinema's capacity to confound objective and subjective events and perspectives. As this film suggests, and many of her subsequent films (*Sweetie, The Piano, Holy Smoke,* and *In the Cut*) confirm, Campion's interest in this phenomenon has less to do with romance and subjective emotion than it does with complicating spectatorial identifications around issues concerning ethics, sexuality, violence, and power—topics I will address in detail in my discussions of these films.

In the first vignette, "Ibrahim Makes Sense of It," the opening shot depicts a chubby man (Elias Ibrahim), his underarm facing the camera, doing side bends, towards and away from the camera, as the narration informs us that "Ibrahim is practicing yoga in his girlfriend's studio. In one of her paintings, there is a sentence, 'Sex is a wonderful and natural thing.'" As the narrator reads, the camera pans across the painting in question, reading it in time with the voiceover. The visuals go back to Ibrahim, bending to the right, as the narrator explains, "As Ibrahim looks to his right, he sees the word 'Sex.'" Cut, as we see the word *Sex*. We see Ibrahim bending to the left, as the narrator tells us and the film shows us that in this direction, Ibrahim sees the word *Thing*. As we get a tight close-up of Ibrahim's face in opaque, black, goggle-like glasses, the narrator tells us, "In his mind, Ibrahim puts the two together: 'sex thing.'" Whereas up to this point, the voiceover has humorously reiterated the content of the images, here the narrator demonstrates his omniscience and reads Ibrahim's mind for us, even as the close-up and Ibrahim's goggles render his expression visually inscrutable.

From this first vignette, *Passionless Moments* goes on to explore its various characters' internal states—memories, fantasies, wishes, regrets, thoughts, and mental speculations—all without the aid of dramatic action or dialogue. Throughout the vignettes, image track and voiceover produce a humorous, profound, and frequently enigmatic sense of the fullness and complexity of any moment. Frequently, two or more vignettes will present variations on the same representational problem, such as "An Exciting One" and "No Woodpeckers in Australia."

"An Exciting One" recounts the fantasy of a boy, Lindsey Aldridge, as he runs home from the store with string beans. The voiceover tells us, "Lindsey imagines that the string beans will explode if he can't get them to his house in twenty seconds." As Lindsey (James Pride) runs, we hear an alarm, getting louder and louder, that sounds exactly like the one at the end of the film *Alien* (1979), warning that the ship is about to blow up. The narrator asks, "Will he make it?" Lindsey runs down the street and into his house as the alarm continues to blare. He closes the door. The alarm continues for two beats then silence.

As spectators, we hear the alarm in three ways, through two different modes whose distinction is consequently muddied: objectively both as a cultural allusion to *Alien* (intended or not) and as a loud sound pervading the mise-en-scène; and subjectively as Lindsey's fantasy, the latter of which we are informed of by the voiceover narration. This vignette works out a provocative parallel between the dramatic appointments that fantasy makes to otherwise mundane aspects of our lives and the dramatic influence that sound effects have on the image. With only voiceover and image, the film would show a boy running home and would tell us the reason, but we would not hear and experience the urgency of his fantasy, conveyed to us by the alarm. The film uses yet innovates the conceit of the deadline by making the imminent crisis all in Lindsey's head. The alarm that we hear is therefore coded as internal diegetic sound—it too is in his head, an experience that the spectator shares with him but that other characters in Lindsey's world cannot. In mimicking *Alien*'s sound effects, the vignette refers to both the power of popular culture to insinuate itself in our fantasy lives and the power and prevalence of intertextual allusions in filmmaking. More importantly, "An Exciting One" aligns us with Lindsey's fantasy through its use of sound effects. Though we hear that alarm objectively, the film dictates that its source is subjective.

A similar experiment with sound structures "No Woodpeckers in Australia," in which the image of Mrs. Gwen Gilbert (Ann Burriman), kneeling on her floor arranging gladiolus in a vase, is accompanied by the sound of wood-tapping-wood that runs throughout the entire vignette. The voiceover narrator recounts Mrs. Gilbert's mental conjectures about the source of the sound—A Japanese woodblock being played in her neighbor's backyard? A woodpecker?—as we see a close-up of her face, skeptically dismissing the first option. As she considers woodpeckers, the film cuts to a cartoon image of a woodpecker pecking on a tree in time to the tapping sound. Cut back to Mrs. Gilbert, who looks out the window and sees her neighbor using a stick to beat a blanket on the clothesline. Along with the tapping of wood on wood, we now can also hear the very different and accurate sound of a stick hitting a blanket. Completely perplexed, Mrs. Gilbert goes back to her flowers while the voiceover states, "Mrs. Gilbert can't understand how Mrs. Veidecheck could make that noise by beating the clothesline with a stick. She reminds herself that we don't have woodpeckers in Australia." In the last shot, we see the animated woodpecker as the tapping finally stops.

"No Woodpeckers" presents a variation on the previous vignette, confounding the question of internal subjective and external objective sound and space through its play with fidelity—the accuracy of a sound in relation to its attributed source in a film. The vignette never definitively locates the source of the animated woodpecker or of the tapping of wood against wood which Mrs. Gilbert can hear, but which, as the film demonstrates, she hears wrongly. The presence of the *proper* sound of wood hitting a blanket leaves wholly unresolved whether this vignette displays Mrs. Gilbert's hallucinatory conjectures (wood-tapping-wood sounds are subjective) and mental images (the cartoon woodpecker) or exemplifies the power of the editing and soundtrack to confound or complicate the sense of a scene for its spectators.

Two similarly paired moments, "A Neighborly Misunderstanding" and "Clear Up Sleepy Jeans" wittily juxtapose two cinematic representations of misinterpretation: the first visual, between two neighbors; the other sonic, a man's belated recognition that he has completely misunderstood the lyrics of a song he had been singing to himself for years. In the first, a shot/reverse shot sequence alternately depicts neighbors Tony Formiati (Alan Brown) and Jim Simpson (Paul Chubb), who have never spoken to one another, each involved in self-grooming activities. Tony, who has had a sports injury, raises his arm as he rubs his shoulder and looks off to the left. The next shot depicts Jim, vigorously brushing something off his neck, looking to the right. Back to Tony, raising his arm, to Jim brushing his neck. In this physical pantomime of mistaken gestures, Tony, the narrator tells us, thinks Jim is waving to him and waves back, thinking that Jim thought he had waved first. In the next shot, we see Jim scurrying off. The camera cuts to a close-up of Tony, as the narrator intones, "Tony realizes some mistake has been made." A lovely play with the conventions of shot/reverse shot and eyeline matches, which conventionally depict characters appearing to see one another, here these shot conventions are used to depict two characters seeing but not understanding what they see at all.

In "Clear Up Sleepy Jeans," by contrast, we see Jim Newbury (Sean Callinan) washing his "smalls" in the bathtub as he sings and hums quietly to himself, "clear up sleepy jeans." The narrator explains that as Jim sings this song from the '70s, now ten years later, he wonders "what this song could possibly mean. For years he's been thinking denim. Could the singer possibly mean to clear up jeans?" As the voiceover narrates Jim's musings, we get a blurred shot of a room with "sleepy" jeans lying all over the bed and on chairs, a shot coded as Jim's speculation. Finally visualizing the sense of the lyrics he's been singing, Jim concludes, "But no, no one would write a song about this, would they?" While continuing to explore *Passionless Moments*' overall project of depicting internal, subjective states, these two vignettes contrast how seeing or hearing or looking at something, either directly or by means of one's imagination, can either confuse or clarify its nature. It is of note that Campion's film depicts the imagination (a vision generated subjectively) as clarifying, whereas what can literally be seen can be completely misunderstood.

Several vignettes address in very different ways the multiple temporalities that memory brings to bear on the moment they present. In "Focal Lengths," an allusion to the past helps rationalize the visual allegory the vignette develops for the gay relationship it depicts. The focal length of a lens is one factor that can determine the depth of field in an individual shot. The opening narration informs us that "Shaun and Arnold aren't speaking. Arnold's mad because Shaun's been playing around," while we see a shot of Arnold (Paul Melchert) in the background, sitting against the wall and Shaun (Yves Stenning) in the foreground, lying with his face toward the camera, both in the sharp, clear focus made possible by a wide-angle lens. Shaun "just can't seem to care. He's wondering why he can't keep two things in focus at the same time," as we see a shot of Shaun, holding his thumb out in front of him, gauging foreground and background, as the focus shifts from his thumb, in the background, to a studded dog collar in the foreground, and back again. Shaun reflects, through the narrator, that "one of these times, it will be all over, but all he can think of now is vague diagrams from school containing focal lengths, umbras, and penumbras."

Shaun's memory of school diagrams, with which the moment ends, presents the "focal length" as the logic for his actions (measuring foreground and background), as an objective correlative for his relationship (he fools around, he can't keep two things in focus at the same time), and as the cinematic logic used to present this vignette, in its altering of deep focus with rack focus. At the level of the voiceover, the focus shifts quickly from Arnold to Shaun and then to what Shaun sees as he considers and then is distracted from the possible end of his relationship. Using an initial, objective shot of the estranged couple, the camera shifts to subjective shots of Shaun's point of view, thereby visually enacting Shaun's inability to keep two things in focus at the same time visually, mentally, and emotionally. These point-of-view shots align the spectator with Shaun and his meditations, a visual alignment enhanced by the explications of the voiceover narrator. "Focal Lengths" thereby pits cinematic identification, cultivated by the narration and the cinematography's focus on Shaun, against a moral identification with Arnold as the injured party, clearly demonstrating the overriding power of the former. Whereas industry cinema's conventionally melodramatic mode typically aligns these two modes of identification, "Focal Lengths" presages Campion's tendency, in her feature films, to complicate the spectators' engagement by splitting and opposing the two.

"Focal Lengths" suggests one function of memory in its witty consideration of how we use concepts and ideas we learned in school in ways for which they were never intended. The next three vignettes, "Angela Eats Meat," "Ed Played Front Row in School," and "What His Mother Said" emphasize, with varying degrees of seriousness, relations between past and present and how film can render the impact of these relations on characters' internal states and emotions. In "Angela Eats Meat," a teenage girl (Sue Collie), waiting for a phone call, lies on the floor and eats slices of cold ham, an activity that provokes her memories of meeting her uncle's pet pig, Rufus. As we see a close-up of a piglet looking directly at the camera, the narrator tells us, "It occurs to her that this is the kind of thinking that turns people vegetarian." We again see Angela in close-up, her ham consumption unabated. The phone rings and she rapidly crawls, on all fours, to get it, as the camera cuts to the pig, wearing a skirt and scurrying away in much the same manner as Angela. As with many other vignettes, the subjective processes depicted in the moment—Angela's memories of Rufus and her agitation about her phone call—are contextualized and subsumed within the film's extradiegetic address to the spectator, here the crosscutting that visually, if also enigmatically, equates Angela with the piglet. Is the object of Angela's attention going to eat her up in much the same way as she eats ham, despite her past affection for Rufus?

From adolescent lust and its perils, the film moves to adult male nostalgia and regret in "Ed Played Front Row at School." Against a backdrop of hanging ironed shirts, Ed (David Benton) in his undershirt, watching the game on TV and drinking a beer, stands at the ironing board while the narrator discloses: "On Sunday, Ed irons six shirts—five for work, one for Saturday night. Ed is off to get himself a fresh beer." In the next shot, Ed walks down a hall, stopping at a window whose view, tellingly, consists entirely of a brick wall. In front of the window, he imagines his old team, looking back at him from under the goal post. He leaps into the air, yelling "Yeah!" and, in a reverse shot, the team leaps up and yells "Yeah!" in answer. The narrator explains, "Ed played front row at school. He wanted to be captain." Ed walks into the kitchen as he remembers a particularly impressive pass he threw. As he faces the camera, fresh beer resting on beer belly, the narrator reveals his thoughts, "Yeah, he's going to give up the grog and get back into training."

Whereas the "yeah" that he exchanges in imagination with his team, remembering times past, was a rallying cry to go out and conquer, the ironic "yeah" of the present is the "yeah" of resolutions that will inevitably not be realized. A subtle and effective visual pun, the image of the brick wall outside the window, represents Ed's prospects and serves as the screen on which he projects himself; altogether it captures the poignant psychology and the material situation of a discouraged bachelor facing middle age.

The next vignette, "What His Mother Said," continues to explore memory and the sad bachelor figure, but from a very different visual and conceptual perspective. The camera, angled downward, tracks around an armchair and out to the middle of a living room floor where a man in a dressing gown is lying face up, staring into space, as we hear a kind of dull throbbing on the soundtrack. The camera then cuts to an overhead close-up of Gavin (George Nezovic), and the narrator tells us, "Gavin Metchalle, bachelor, has been trying to put his life together for three or four years. At the moment, he is listening to the beat of his own eardrums. As this fades from his attention, he notices particles of lint drifting through the air in front of his eyes." The camera cuts to the lint and then to Gavin, looking up at it as we hear, "He watches the lint for a moment, remembering his mother used to tell him they were angels."

"What His Mother Said" replaces brick wall with the sound of throbbing eardrums and a vision of swirling lint. Back to back, the two vignettes distinguish working-class masculine ennui from its middle-class, or even affluent, variant by mobilizing material objects—TV, beer, brick wall or armchair, silk dressing gown, and lint—whose realistic function gives rise to a rich network of connotations and symbols. Insofar as the film seeks to depict the concrete materiality of any given moment, it also explores how that materiality can suggest lyrical abstractions about class and its real and psychological implications (Ed must work six days a week, whereas Gavin has time to be enthralled with lint, etc).

Passionless Moments culminates with "Scotties, Part of the Grand Design of the Universe." Focusing on Julie Fry (Rebecca Stewart), a young girl in goggles making truck noises and playing in a very messy bedroom (she's home "sick" from school), this vignette recounts how Julie accidentally discovers that Monopoly money fits perfectly on the back of a Scotties box. As with any significant discovery, this one leads to further research as Julie tries other paper products on the Scotties box—"her exercise book—no, but folded in half they would." The narrator tells us that Julie "pictures a large conference room where men in suits discuss the proportions of paper" as we see in long shot a group of men in dress shirts, sitting around a large conference table, folding paper and putting it on Scotties boxes. Julie goes on to drink tea out of a toy cup, her goggles reminiscent of Ibrahim in the vignette which opens the film. Over this shot, the narrator ties up the film, remarking, "We leave Julie now as her moment passes. There are one million moments in your neighborhood, but as the filmmakers discovered, each has a fragile presence, which fades almost as it forms."

Passionless Moments brilliantly counterpoises the poignant subjective content of its voiceover with the narrator's wry tone of voice and the film's arch cinematography, both meta-narrative structures that let the film have its pathos while ironizing it too. As with *Mishaps* and *Peel*, Campion and Lee use sophisticated cinematic techniques to map the film's wit directly onto its most effective evocations of pain, boredom, loss, and miscommunication. *Passionless Moments* also demonstrates, perhaps even more effectively than *Mishaps* and *Peel*, Campion's interest in and ability to represent damaged masculinity and its travails, though some of this film's power must certainly be attributed to Lee.

Story

Instead of focusing on ten moments representing a Sydney neighborhood's million, *A Girl's Own Story* (1984) precisely dates and locates the traumatic family and social experiences of three teenage girls, Pam, Stella, and Gloria, within white middle- to working-class youth culture of 1960s Australia. Campion's final student film, *A Girl's Own Story*, brings together the concerns (dysfunctional families, sibling rivalry, erotic triangulation, adult's abuse of children) and techniques (blurring of objective and subjective states, combining of documentary and surreal filmic modes, graphic matches and elliptical editing, the use of visual puns) of the earlier three in the most sustained and complex narrative of her student work. As in *Peel* and *Passionless Moments*, the film's interests include the ethnographic (in its investigation of Australian adolescent girls) and the traumatic (in its focus on familial dysfunction). Like *Mishaps* and *Peel*, siblings (two sisters and a brother and sister, all adolescents) are crucial to the plot, and at the heart of the story are two very disturbed families. In visuals and structure, *A Girl's Own Story* provides an apt companion piece to *Passionless Moments*, its black-and-white cinematography pushing the expressionist and frequently surreal visual flourishes of the earlier film even farther. The film's narrative proceeds by loosely stringing together various brilliantly conceived set pieces, not unlike the vignettes of the previous film, save the same characters recur. It captures the lives of its adolescent protagonists by pointed references to Beatlemania as well as to what one reviewer referred to as "the Antipodean inflections" throughout, one of which, "the two-bar electric fires," does double duty as a specific cultural reference and as one crucial part of the film's symbolic structure, which is discussed in the following paragraph (Glaessner 209). Thus this film, like her first three, demonstrates Campion's proclivity to blend an ethnographic impulse and precision with surreal visualizations of (what might be) character's subjective states, this blend thereby registering but transcending the focus on individual characters that dominates industry cinema. Finally, it bears mention that this is the first of her films to single out girls and women as its particular subject.

The ambivalent significations that open *A Girl's Own Story* refer to the range and mode of mixed messages adolescent girls confronted during the 1960s. Following three tight close-ups of the main characters, accompanied by a music box rendition of "Lara's Theme" (a song that saturated global culture with 1965's epic *Doctor Zhivago*), we see a book page, illustrated with the profile of a naked man. One of the girls runs her finger along this profile, tracing the outline of the man's large erect penis, and then underlines the illustration's caption: "This sight may shock young girls." The collision/collusion of treacly romantic music with a biology textbook's rhetoric of sexual threat—pointedly not intended for young girls to read but the type of book that every teenager manages to find—captures that era's highly problematic practice of inundating girls with sentimental tales of romance while withholding basic information about sex (Bloustein 3). The film's title, which appears next, seems to emphasize the story as a possession of one single girl, but the subsequent shots, of Catholic school girls generic in their uniforms, visually represents "girls" as plural, the inference being that all these girls have their own stories, both individuated and, yet, in an ethnographic sense, all versions of the same story.

Having introduced the romance/sex distinction under the rubrics of treacle and threat, the film then explores the girls', especially Pam's (Gabrielle Shomegg) attempts to "find a place," a "somewhere" that eludes all of them. Places and people from whom one might expect support—school and friends, home, parents and siblings—prove to be unreliable at best, manipulative or vicious at worst. Pam's mother (Colleen Fitzpatrick) is severely depressed, her father (Paul Chubb) narcissistic and dishonest. Her sister wants to kill her for wearing her white go-go boots and actually threatens her with a knife. One friend, Stella (Geraldine Haywood), dumps her for a different social clique at school, and the other, Gloria (Marina Knight), gets pregnant by her own brother Graeme (John Godden) and has to go away to an unwed mothers' home. While this plot summary might read as a very melodramatic coming-of-age narrative, its filmic realization avoids pathos, registering instead as analytical and often darkly comic; in so doing, it astutely approximates in tone the quality of adolescent alienation.

Two early scenes demonstrate this visual and affective alienation. Pam and Stella appear at Pam's house after school, and over a shot of two space heaters (the "two-bar electric fires"), glowing and clanking, we hear Pam remark, "I guess she's home somewhere." The next several shots depict Pam's interaction with her mother. In the first, we see a small room, shot with a wide-angle lens in depth, one end of it shrouded in darkness, the other where Pam's mother sits, her face in shadow. Over these noirish visuals, we hear, faintly, the dialogue of a TV soap opera. Pam's mother turns her head as the camera cuts to Pam's face in the doorway. Pam tells her mother, "Stella's staying for tea, OK?" Back to her mother, who says nothing, just stares blankly. The camera cuts to a close-up of her hand, as she arches her palm then flattens it in her lap. Pam, exasperated, shuts the door. This sequence brilliantly captures the quality of the mother's mute yet profound depression and her daughter's extreme frustration and anger at her. It frames both within its implicit critique of soap operas, a sentimental, domestic discourse directed to women that also mystifies sex and romance in its treatment of "women's issues," and avoids nondramatic problems like depression. Campion transforms the domestic maternal melodrama scenario rendered by her own film, visualizing it as suffused with confusion and menace, by employing the expressionistic shadows and cinematography of film noir.

In this scene and throughout the film, the cinematography, lighting, framing, and blocking visually convey "the very texture of uncertainty and insecurity" (Robson and Zalcock 42). Yet the film carefully avoids cultivating audience identification with its characters through its use of shadows, cramped shots (Pam's face in close-up, squeezed between the doorframe and the door as she talks to her mother), and timing. Campion consistently holds shots in this film longer than necessary, letting the silence and the frozen poses of the characters both impress themselves on us visually and make us uncomfortable. Yet she also employs a very pronounced visual wit, nuancing the grimness of *A Girl's Own Story* with an ironic narrational perspective. In the next scene, Pam and Stella go to Pam's room, kiss pictures of the Beatles on the wall and then each other, with Pam wearing a Beatles mask but not Stella, so it won't "be like two blokes kissing." As they make out in the background of the shot, the camera pans over a long line of Barbie dolls and we again hear "Lara's Theme." The ludicrous yet somehow exactly accurate incongruity of it all—the dolls, the song, the necking—is reiterated by the awkward physicality, the almost dutiful nature of the kissing. Pam, lying on top of Stella, inadvertently pulls her hair, and sits up when Stella complains. When Pam asks Stella if what they are doing is OK, she responds that "it's just practice for later, not like what Gloria and her brother did." When Pam asks her what she means, Stella replies that it was "just something Gloria said."

The sequences that follow alternate between Pam's difficulties and Gloria's, recounting each with the compression Campion demonstrated in *Passionless Moments*. The tea at Pam's house, to which Stella is invited, demonstrates, through visuals and dialogue, the highly dysfunctional dynamics of Pam's family. Pam's parents, at opposite ends of the table, flanked by Pam on one side, her sister (Joanne Gabbe) and Stella on the other, are not speaking (and haven't spoken for two years, we learn a bit later). Following this establishing shot, the subsequent conversation is rendered by medium shots of each individual, either as they speak or listen, with the camera in a direct line in front of them. Lit harshly, with the background plunged in shadows, each character is completely visually isolated, with Campion pointedly avoiding the shot reverse shots or eyeline matches that would place them in relation to one another.

The dialogue begins with Pam's father flirtatiously complimenting Stella on her "lovely" and "fetching" curls. He then says to Pam, "Tell your mother she ought to get a curling wand." Dad then flirts with his wife, using his daughter as a conduit, telling Pam to "tell her that dress is gorgeous," which Pam significantly repeats as, "He said to tell you that dress is nice." Pam speaks slowly and loudly to her mother, enunciating as if her mother is hard of hearing. In a reestablishing shot, we see the entire table, Pam spatially positioned, as she is emotionally, between her "absent" and withholding mother and her manipulative and inappropriate father. Upping the sexual ante, Dad looks in his wife's direction and says appreciatively of her dress, "You've got the legs for those minis," which draws an anxious protest from Pam's sister, "It's not a mini!" Pam dutifully begins to shout to her mother, "He says to tell you you've got the legs . . ." when, finally roused, her mother interrupts, yelling, "Oh God, I can hear him. Ask him where he was last night so late." When Pam's sister confronts her father with her mother's question, he yells at her for wearing a stocking on her head at the table and both she and her mother run out of the room.

The scene takes another turn as Pam says, "Jesus, Dad, why'd you let her do it? Humiliate us like that?!"—an interpretation of what we have just seen clearly distorted by her rage at her mother. Turning to (and on) her, Dad upbraids Pam immediately, saying, "Don't talk about your mother like that—she's a wonderful woman . . . she's my wife and I love her." The dialogue, character blocking, and cinematography of this scene concretize the pathological dynamics of dysfunctional families, wherein children serve as translators, conduits, and targets for their parents' aggressions, desires, and ambivalence for one another. In the space of this short scene, Pam is not only used, but is alternately emotionally solicited and rejected by both parents. The sympathy we feel for her, her mother, and her sister is complicated by their complicity in these dynamics (which the film clearly establishes) and also by the fact that the table and conversation are lit and shot, with bright light and dark shadows, like an interrogation scene.

Later, Stella snubs Pam at the pool after gym class; Pam, in the foreground of the shot, is awkward in her towel, while in the background, Stella huddles with her friends. Pam's sister creeps into her room at night, brandishing a knife, after which we see a sequence which might be Pam's memory or a nightmarish dream. A younger Pam, walking down the street in the dark, is lured into a car by a man who entices her with his kitten. We never see his face, only his black leather gloves holding the kitten, but in the palpable dissonance between leather and fur, his big hands and the tiny kitten, Campion materially conveys, in a way that the audience can tactilely experience, the creepiness and horror of the situation. Finally, as at the dinner table, her father betrays Pam twice,

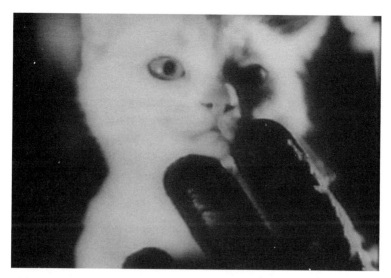

Leather glove and kitten; sexual threat in
A Girl's Own Story

first by asking his mistress to come along to her special birthday dinner with him and second by ending a physical altercation with her mother in a passionate embrace. The two fall to the floor, oblivious to their surroundings, as Pam, distressed and shaken, rapidly crawls up the stairs while her older sister laughs at her, saying, "They're only having sex."

A Girl's Own Story tells of incest, family strife, and possibly molestation by a stranger, presenting repeated instances where sexual menace and desire are tangled and confused with one another, a motif that runs through many of Campion's feature films. The romantic naivete and optimism of the epic and pop love songs with which the film begins—"Lara's Theme" and "I Should Have Known Better"—are answered by the bleak realism of the one with which it ends, "Feel the Cold," whose lyrics were penned by Campion. This ending reiterates the ambivalence of *A Girl's Own Story*'s opening, with the terms converted to express the character of the girls' alienation. In a dark, otherwise empty room, not motivated by or integrated within the narrative, we see a deep focus shot of electric heaters, each of the girls (Pam, her sister, and Stella) sitting next to one and singing "Feel the Cold." As the camera moves from one girl to another, we see a shot of a girl ice skating, just her feet spinning on the ice, superimposed on their faces. With its use of black-and-white cinematography, wide-angle lenses, awkward framings, frozen poses, and lengthy silences, the film keeps the temperature down, all the characters' lack of empathy and understanding for each other blending with the heat of their erotic and sadistic impulses toward one another. The film's dominant organization is narrative, but a narrative less causal than stylistically and thematically associative. Finally, our affective engagement with *A Girl's Own Story* is both perceptive and cold, acute and distanced, a paradox that echoes the characters' feelings toward one another—ambivalent, hot and cold, seductive and alienated.

Present in these early films are insistent images and motifs that will recur throughout Campion's oeuvre—an obsession with tactility, with hands and fingers, their capabilities, their menace, and their possible loss (*Mishaps, A Girl's Own Story, The Piano, The Portrait of a Lady, Holy Smoke, In the Cut*); an interest in siblings (*Mishaps, Peel, A Girl's Own Story, Sweetie, Angel at My Table, Holy Smoke, In the Cut*); and detached mothers and seductive and inappropriate fathers (*A Girl's*

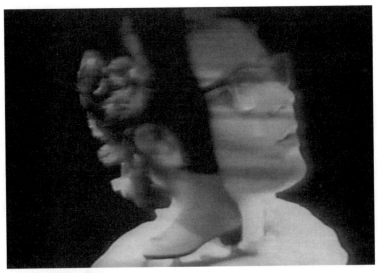

Feel the cold: ice skates in *A Girl's Own Story*

Own Story, Sweetie, The Portrait of a Lady, Holy Smoke, In the Cut). The focus on desire, ice, burning, and freezing that shapes *Mishaps's* tale of two adult brothers reappears in *A Girl's Own Story's* account of adolescent sisters and friends and, again, in *In the Cut's* narrative of two adult sisters. In addition, the two latter films' structural and thematic similarities are tellingly conveyed by the ice and ice skates that end the earlier film and that open the fantasy structure of the later one.

All of the complexity of Campion's later feature films is present in these early films, from her knowing appropriations and remotivations of melodramatic conventions to her proclivity for a surreal visual field.[13] Her visual imagination, lush, tactile, and sensuous, is shot through with an ethnographer's investment in apt, characteristic detail, just as her interest in the "nasty" side of things—dysfunctional families, child abuse, depressed and negligent mothers, seductive fathers, murderous siblings, sexual violence, and death—is blended with a sophisticated and wholly unsentimental wit. Campion's sustained investigation of the surreal, the permeability of objective and subjective cinematic representation, allows for the coexistence of this darkness and wit; she gives us dazzling insights into her characters while keeping her narration and our perspective distant, frequently amused, and ironic. In her early films, men, women, and children all share focus, though *A Girl's Own Story* does signal the unique nonjudgmental perspective Campion will later bring to her feature narratives grappling with "women's issues" such as incest, unwanted pregnancy, single motherhood, sexual violence, and depression.

In dealing with these issues, Campion sets women's desire in tension with their agency, frequently realizing her characters' conflicts with themselves and with others through an ongoing motif of bad choices. As Amy Taubin put it in her review of *In the Cut*, "Women who choose the wrong man is one of [Campion's] basic themes as are the inseparable connection between sex and power and the potentially devastating contradictions between rationality and unconscious desire" (52). The motif of the bad or wrong choice, the conflict between body and will, reason and desire, are all concerns which have drawn the interest and the ire of Campion's feminist viewers and critics.

Film Feature Narration and a New Kind of Feminism

Campion's feature films emerged from an array of influences and experiences that included formal training in anthropology, the arts, and film, and from a historical moment permeated by feminism that shaped the antipodean industry in which she would come of age. In her theatrically released features, she has repeatedly taken up the conventions of industry cinema and recognizable mainstream genres, revisioning them through the use of surrealist and ethnographic techniques. Campion's originality or distinction derives from her deft synthesis of the multiple influences on her filmmaking, a synthesis that facilitated the crossover phenomenon of *The Piano*, a "popular" film with an edgy art cinema take on sexuality and violence.

The specifics of this synthesis are evident in her complex narrational strategies. Moving from short films to feature narration, Campion continued to use many formal techniques, such as voiceover narration and eccentric framing and cutting, as well as to focus on topics having to do with sexual and familial trauma. Within the enlarged narrative context of the feature film, the latter begs the question of genre. Insofar as all her features foreground female protagonists who suffer the effects of personal trauma, they share the generic concerns of family melodramas or women's films. Further, Campion's consistent use of highly significant objects, colors, and detail in mise-en-scène and of spectacle, suspense, and dramatic plot reversals in her narratives partake of the larger sense of melodrama, what Linda Williams has characterized as "a fundamental mode" of popular American film and mass culture overall (12–13). This mode generates spectacles of virtuous suffering to speak the "unspeakable," to foster the reader/spectator's identification with what Peter Brooks calls "moral legibility" through the recounting of an innocent victim's travails.

Campion, although clearly adopting the concerns of the family or woman's melodrama in all her films, and the cinematic rhetoric of this pervasive industry mode in many of them, pointedly avoids one crucial feature of both. She refuses to portray her female protagonists as victims, no matter how harrowing the dilemmas they face, and she never allows her spectacles of suffering to operate in the service of moral revelation. Although she cultivates affective responses to her films through conventionally melodramatic means— music, aspects of mise-en-scène—she makes use of various strategies and alternative representational modes, such as surrealism and ethnography, to preclude that affective engagement from becoming a moral, sentimental identification with her characters. She does this in four ways.

First, Campion does not present vulnerability as exclusive to women and children. She renders femininity and childhood in relation to equally complex representations of often vulnerable masculinity. She features men as well as women in pain, cuckolded, humiliated, or abject. Indeed, as in *Mishaps*, her plots often involve power struggles between women and men, in which the characters' power and positions blur and switch. Of Ada and Stewart (Sam Neill) in *The Piano*, she says, "In the story, men are seen as objects: it's a bit of a role reversal. I think it's amusing because more often you see women who are looking for an emotional relationship with men, while men think only about sex. Here, Ada is the one who has an erotic temperament, which is interesting" (Wexman, *Interviews*, 130). At the same time, however, her narratives do not fail to underscore that the power to which men and women have access (physical strength, political, legal, and social positioning) is not commensurate and that any reversals of their positions are necessarily asymmetrical. She distinguishes her storytelling from that of mainstream film by refusing to *moralize* that incommensurability.

Second, Campion's narration routinely exercises and integrates a shared representational concern of cinematic melodrama and surrealism: both are different ways of visualizing what isn't there, what can't be seen. Melodrama customarily relies on elements of mise-en-scène to convey character expression and to "externalize the inner states of characters" (Gledhill 23). Its spectacle thereby precipitates the merger of sympathetic feeling and moral revelation characteristic of this mode, making visible the intensification of social relations in excesses of mise-en-scène. Here, the visual field evokes the (invisible) affective state of its characters to provoke that state in its spectators, one infused with ideological import.

Alternately, surrealism seeks to visualize the irruption of the unconscious and the irrational in everyday life and to immerse its spectator in the shocking, capricious, or uncanny experience of that irruption. The unseeable, unspeakable, makes itself felt in the "return of the repressed" in the diegetic field, a field whose status as objective or subjective reality is put into question for its spectator. Campion systematically suspends clear distinctions between objective and subjective viewpoints, as in *Mishaps*, when George or Geoffrey's inner voice (their letters) are visually represented by found newsreel footage, or in *Girl's Own*, when we see young Pam being abducted, but cannot be certain whether this footage is the film's representation of an actual event, of Pam's memory, or of a nightmare she is having. Campion thereby maps onto the affective diffusions of melodrama the perceptual confusions of the surreal. The visual field of her films is often distorted by tight or eccentric framings, wide-angle lenses, persistent shadows, and other techniques that distort or limit or confuse our perspective on the action. These surreal framings visualize character affect and transform it into spectators' perceptual disorientation within the diegesis overall. Thus instead of identifying and sympathizing with individual characters, spectators experience perceptually the effects of traumas whose nature or exact causes the films frequently withhold from us.

Third, Campion refuses to engage in the moral/utopian gestures of either the melodramatic or the surreal (the latter's subjectification of the text to the unconscious) through her use of ethnography. The music employed in her films is particularly telling in this regard. In another remotivation of melodramatic convention, Campion frequently constructs her soundtracks from compelling songs that do not accompany the visuals to which they are applied so much as comment ironically on them. She selects songs from various genres (gospel, pop, bebop, traditional) that cannot be fully appropriated to the dramatic situation to which they are applied because of significant temporal, geographical, cultural, or religious disjunctions between the two. Although the music operates as an emotional lure for spectators, the oddity of its use is also quite apparent. This disjunction either "dates" the spectator's experience or otherwise emphasizes the historical and cultural specificity of her narratives.

Finally, while Campion's films do tell stories, their elliptical structure links fragmentary moments based on a logic of association as often as of causality. Frequently her opening sequences introduce master motifs (trees in *Sweetie*, fingers in *The Piano*) that have structural and meta-narrative, as well as thematic, import. She often eschews logical or rational motivations for characters' actions and behavior, instead exploring figural or visual motivations such as mimicry. As articulated by the surrealists, mimicry derived from the reversibility of the visual dynamic (seeing and being seen) and its relation to projection and desire. Her films are filled with characters who imitate each other, in direct pantomimes, or who are visual as well as thematic doubles. Some of her characters, such as the woman writer in *Mishaps*, are subject to mimetic infection or contagion,[14] which could be defined as "a subject that is dispossessed within its very being by the fact of being seen or desired" (Krauss 82).[15] Related to mimetic infection is Campion's sustained exploration of masochism and its relation of reversibility with sadism (Freud 23–26). She works with paradoxes of relation—desire is a force that freezes as well as burns, love is sometimes inextricable from hate, sadism and masochism revert back and forth to one another. These paradoxes of relation take place in the context of a crucial concern: (female) agency and desire and the irrational status of choice for characters compelled by both. Campion's films attempt to implicate spectators in this dilemma, one with ethical and emotional dimensions, through her narration's insinuations of melodramatic, surrealist, and ethnographic techniques and structures of identification.

As these remarks might suggest, Campion has had a very complicated relationship with feminism. The film that brought her international renown, *The Piano* (1993), also generated intense and dramatically polarized debate, especially among women, about its feminist implications or the lack thereof. Although some found the film a mesmerizing and masterful depiction of a decidedly female sensibility and sexuality, others asserted that it rendered abuse and rape in the worst possible way as Ada, the "victim," ends up loving and running off with Baines, one of the men who abuses her.[16] All of Campion's films focus on women's encounters with power, violence, and abuse, together with complex structures of narration, characterization, and plot development that thwart easy or unambiguous interpretation. In their resolute refusal to moralize these encounters, Campion's films can be seen as timely enactments of analogous developments of feminist theory in the '90s.

Though writing on feminist politics rather than aesthetics, Wendy Brown articulates the nature of the challenges to feminism that I argue are posed by Campion's films: "The question is whether feminist politics can prosper without a moral apparatus, whether feminist theorists and activists will give up substituting Truth and Morality for politics. Are we willing to engage in struggle rather than recrimination, to develop our faculties rather than avenge our subordination with moral and epistemological gestures, to fight for a world rather than conduct process on the existing one?" (48).

In her call for feminists to "give up substituting Truth and Morality for politics," Brown refers to the Nietzschean concept of *ressentiment*, which refers to the "morality that emerges from the powerless to avenge their incapacity for action; it enacts their resentment of strengths that they cannot match or overthrow" (44). *Ressentiment* invokes the "good" and the "true" as judgment and weapon against such strengths and thereby ascends to power over it on the basis of morality rather than deeds. Brown, quoting Foucault, argues that feminist politics could avoid *ressentiment* by forgoing "specifically *moral* claims against domination [. . .] and moving instead into the domain of the sheerly political: 'wars of position' and amoral contests about the just and the good in which truth is always grasped as coterminous with power, as always already power, as the voice of power" (45).

Brown's call speaks to the dynamics of the tales Campion tells, tales in which neither her heroines nor the films themselves resort to frameworks of truth or morality to make sense of the struggles with domination the heroines experience and the films recount. Though her films reference certain genealogies and pasts—whether familial, colonial, or generic—they noticeably refuse the conventional relations usually articulated between past and present in these milieu.[17] Instead, chronicling her characters' struggles with and attitudes toward adversity, she mixes an ethnographic curiosity with surrealist wit and tragic irony. Significantly this approach in Campion's films coincides with some form of voiceover narration—sometimes female, sometimes not—that exists in tension with the films' other structures of narration. The perspective that emerges is consequently plural, ambiguous, and difficult for spectators to assume in an unproblematic way. She uses formal means of narration to insert meta-narrative commentary, evident both in her selection of diegetic and nondiegetic music and in the form of surreal or darkly comic visual puns that both resonate with and complicate the voice(s) of her character-narrators. The "female narration" in Campion's films emerges from these interactions between the character-narrators and the film's formal narration and meta-narrative strategies that are then critically comprehended and vested in the name and persona of "Jane Campion." Focusing on the interplay between the embodied and formal narration within the films themselves, I will consider how this interplay creatively explores the possibility of an engaged feminine/feminist perspective outside of "a moral apparatus" and focused on "struggle" rather than pathos or "recrimination" as feminist modalities. The development of this perspective is apparent in *Sweetie* (1989), Campion's first feature released in the United States.

Sweetie: Sisters and Family Trees

Sweetie recounts a family "coming apart like a wet paper bag." It is the father (Jon Darling) of the family who speaks this line, a father who has a highly inappropriate relationship with one of his two daughters, one that perhaps was incestuous when she was young. The film never lets us know what really happened in the past but rather focuses on the family in the present. Our access to this family comes through the other daughter, Kay (Karen Colston), who narrates its opening section.

The film begins with sound before the image. Over a black screen, we hear a singer from the Australian Café at the Gates of Salvation choir intone: "Somebody told me about an endless journey. I feel it clearly now." As the song continues, ominous chords slowly overwhelm it, and, from an overhead camera angle in the film's first shot, we see two feet in the middle of the frame splayed against a gaudy leaf- and floral-patterned carpet. The camera cuts back and moves around to reveal Kay, her elbow over her eyes, as we hear her saying in voiceover:

> We had a tree in our yard with a palace in the branches. It was built for my sister and had fairy lights that went on and off in sequence. She was a princess. It was her tree. She wouldn't let me up it. At night, the darkness frightens me. Someone could be watching from behind the trees, someone who wishes you harm. I used to imagine the roots of that tree, crawling, crawling right under the house, right under the bed. Maybe that's why trees scare me. It's like they have hidden powers.

With this provocative speech, the narrative begins. The voiceover signals the concerns and the organization of the film to follow by its shifts in focus and tense that move from narrator Kay's experience with her sister in the past to her phobias in the present. Campion and cowriter Gerald Lee employ the three-part story arc beloved of Hollywood screenwriting, but instead of patterning *Sweetie* on rising and falling dramatic action, they use distinct shifts in narration, music, and character focus to fashion a quasi-(psycho)analysis of a dysfunctional family. The clearly neurotic Kay, whose phobias and superstitions instigate the film's romantic plot— her coupling with boyfriend Louis (Tom Lycos)—narrates the opening third. Close to thirty minutes into the film, the sudden appearance of Kay's sister (the eponymous Sweetie [Geneviève Lemon]) and then parents (Flo [Dorothy Barry] and Gordon) sets Kay's fears and emotional and sexual constriction in the externalized context of her family romance. In this second section, the fragments of familial interactions that we see in the present compel us to speculate on the family's past, a past that the film alludes to but never fully reveals. About a half hour later, the narrative shifts again, as Louis, Kay, and Gordon leave Sweetie behind and set off to join Flo, who has invited them to the outback where she is working. In this third section, travel and movement signal a transformation in the family dynamics as a consequence of the mother's actions. A catastrophe ensues (Sweetie dies). Two separate sequences end the film, the first narrated by and depicting Kay in the present and the second, from Gordon's perspective, rendering Sweetie in the past.

The first third of the film sets Kay's subjective narration, conveyed by her dreams and mental states, point of view shots, and voiceover, in the context of highly ironic plot machinations and uses of music. The plot is initially motivated by Kay's superstitious magical thinking, while the film style—off-center framings, noncontinuity editing, and highly noticeable independent camera movement—presents a surreal visual world, both mundane and ominous, that matches its protagonist's neurotic sensibility.[18] These qualities are evident in the film's opening sequences.

In a lateral tracking shot, we see Kay walking down the street, her erratic gait revealed by a subsequent high-angle point-of-view shot to be a result of her refusal to step on any of the many cracks in the sidewalk. She stands before a door, and, in the next shot, sits at a psychic's

(Jean Hadgraft) dining table next to the psychic's severely autistic adult son (Paul Livingston), getting her tea leaves read. Shots of the psychic centered in the frame alternate with those of Kay and the son: Kay dour and plaintive; the son rocking, grimacing, and physically agitated. Looking at the tea leaves in Kay's cup, the psychic sees a man, "offering a deep love," with a question mark on his face. The dark claustrophobic apartment with its lurid floral wallpaper and tacky bric-a-brac, the son's abnormality and his mother's clairvoyance, and her vision of a man and a question mark in the soggy leaves in a teacup evince the uncanny juxtapositions of surrealism even as they register, in astute ethnographic detail, the convenient home employment of a working-class widow in Sydney caring for her disabled son.

In having the psychic's prediction simply transform Kay's question about her future into a literal question mark inscribed on a man's face, the screenwriters wittily capture the projective character of the occult. The question becomes the answer as what is desired within becomes what will arrive from without. The film also employs what the surrealists called "objective chance" as a plot device. Objective chance occurs when external reality produces an object or "verbal fragment" that a

Kay's feet and cracks in the sidewalk in *Sweetie* |

person reads as a magical sign of one's own desire (Krauss 35). In the very next sequence, Kay does indeed meet a man, Louis, with a question mark on his forehead (formed by a curl and a mole), who has just gotten engaged to one of her coworkers. She meets him secretly in a parking garage, notably in section 13, telling him that they are "destined" to be together and that she is as surprised as he is at this turn of events. They agree to toss five coins "for keeps" that have to be all tails. They are. Seduced by chance rather than by choice, the two kiss and fall to the ground in a passionate embrace, as we hear the choir singing: "I'm on the right road to glory." A subsequent shot shows Louis and Kay in a bedroom, apparently postcoital, as the choir harmonizes: "Love will never, never, never let you fall." The screen goes to black, with a title, "13 months later."

In these opening sequences, the film constructs its romantic plot (man with a question mark), delimits its timeline (13 months), and selects its music (choir) according to different belief systems—objective chance, superstition, magical thinking, religion—whose projective logics it self-consciously employs. By beginning its plot where conventional romances usually end—with the successful creation of the couple against seemingly insurmountable odds—the film signposts its intention to "go beyond" the dictates of industry cinema narratives. The typical melodrama of the rival and unrequited love is summarily and amorally upended with five tosses of a coin and the disappearance of Louis's fiancée. *Sweetie* pursues "happily ever after" thirteen months later.

As critics have noted, "Superstition and mysticism control Kay's life" (Bloustien 7), and her proclivity for the occult is aligned with her familial trauma.[19] Yet as with Campion's short films, Kay's dysfunctional orientation is integrated within larger social trends and groups, giving an ethnographic inflection to her story. The choir music, which runs all through the first third of *Sweetie*, is of a piece with the other references to chance—spirituality, mysticism, and sexuality—that make up the somewhat desultory narrative of Louis and Kay's domestic and romantic life. Louis meditates while Kay shows Clayton (Andre Pataczek), the five-year-old boy who lives next door, her tiny china horses, treasured keepsakes from her childhood. Kay, somewhat resentfully, goes to transcendental meditation classes. While she is in class, another woman, Melony, shows Louis a book on tantric sex, clearly making a play for him. When Louis and Kay stop having sex despite attempts to schedule a time for it, they muse that their relationship is more spiritual, and that the Dalai Lama doesn't "do it."

The non-diegetic choir and character references to the Dalai Lama and tantric sex perform several crucial functions in relation to Louis and Kay's romance. At the same time that the religious lyrics of the choir music objectively express the subjective hope and feelings of redemption that often accompany sexual love and passion, their coincidence ("I'm on the right road to glory" as the two commence their road to coitus) is apt, amusing, and oddly dissonant. This use of music calls attention to the significant overlap between sexuality and spirituality as systems of belief whose convergence has marked western (counter)culture since the 1960s.

The film also demonstrates, whether intentionally or not, that this convergence is animated by appropriations of cultural and racial difference. The "spiritual" frames of reference Kay and Louis use to make sense of and compensate for their sexual problems blend western superstition with Asian religious figures and practices. Thus Kay and Louis represent a familiar ethnotype (to much of the film's intended audience) whose reliance on the occult, on the irrational, on spiritual analogies—tea leaves, coin tosses, and the Dalai Lama's celibacy—is infused with unacknowledged, secularized, and medicinal incorporations of cultural and racial otherness. This theme, a marginalized concern in *Sweetie*, will recur in Campion's work, most notably in *Holy Smoke*, as will her tendency to use music for objective as well as subjective signification; that is, not only as affective cue, but as critical or ethnographic commentary to compel spectators to make associations that complicate and broaden the meaning of what we are seeing.[20]

Along these same lines, two highly subjective sequences in this early section relay Kay's morbid fear of trees through film footage derived from pointedly objective sources. The night that Louis plants a baby elder tree (the mixed generational reference in "baby elder" is surely not accidental) in honor of their relationship, Kay has a nightmare, visually conveyed by 1950s black-and-white newsreel footage of men planting a tree, together with time-lapse cinematography depicting a plant sprouting and breaking through dirt and concrete. Horrified, she wakes up, walks outside, and pulls up the sapling, hiding it in the wardrobe of the spare room where she spends the rest of the night. She tells Louis she has a cold and then doesn't move back to their bedroom even after her cold goes away. Similarly, in her TM class, she closes her eyes and a rapid montage depicts her mind racing with images: the question mark on Louis's forehead, a real question mark, dirt spilling out of the wardrobe where she has hidden the uprooted sapling, a large tree, a girl's feet dancing in white socks, and tree roots. As Campion did in *Mishaps* and will do in *Portrait*, here she employs "objective" film sources—newsreel, scientific, and documentary film footage—to present highly subjective material. Surreal in expression, this combination works to objectify or render strange Kay's sensibilities while also effectively expressing her affect.

Kay is terrified of trees, of roots, of what is beneath and behind trees, of what you can't see. In short, she is afraid of the back story, of her family tree. Through her, in the film's opening voiceover and visuals (the gaudy leaf carpet), Campion puts a genealogical metaphor, the family tree, into play to tell an alternative story about the familial projections that shape and haunt romance. Trees won't leave Kay alone. In a fairy-tale logic (or that of the psychoanalytic return of the repressed), the uprooted baby elder draws to it exactly what she means to keep at bay.[21] As she and Louis return home one night, ominous music plays on the soundtrack. They discover their front window smashed and find that Sweetie (who Kay initially identifies as "a friend of mine" who's "a bit mental") has broken into their house. Sweetie is with Bob (Michael Lake), a heroin addict whom she refers to as her show-business manager.

With Sweetie's arrival, the narration of the film changes. Kay's voiceover disappears, as does the gospel music, neither of which we will hear again until Kay's coda at the end of the film. From an ironic focus on Kay's inner world, we move to her perceptions of and reactions to her sister Sweetie. The extreme off-center framing and cutting of the film's opening section and its lack of dramatic action readily conveyed Kay's neurosis; once Sweetie appears in the second section, however, the style of the film becomes less noticeably strange, emphasizing Sweetie's bizarre behavior as an externalized complement to the strangeness of Kay's inner world.

The film highlights the complementary construction of the sisters in other ways as well. Whereas Kay is introduced by voiceover and music, Sweetie's character emerges through her actions (breaking into her sister's house) and the telling (and hilarious) dialogue that takes place about that between her and her sister. When Kay rages at her for breaking the window in the door, Sweetie replies, "It wouldn't open, Kay; it was really stiff." Kay responds, "Of course it was, it was locked." Breaking down doors becomes a motif for Sweetie when she tells Kay, with a line she will repeat several times, "Bob and I are really going to walk through some doors, Kay. We're really getting it together." Encouraged by her father's fantasies of her talent when she was young (the dancing feet we've seen in Kay's meditation are Sweetie's feet), Sweetie aspires to make it as an actress and entertainer. The film makes it clear that what talent Sweetie has is limited to an acrobatic stunt with chairs and the most basic of dance moves. What she does have is a gift for acting out, with Kay as her favored target. She wreaks havoc in her sister's household, having loud sex with Bob in the living room, coming on to Louis, telling everyone lies, cutting up Kay's dresses and dyeing them, and, in a delirium of rage, chewing on Kay's tiny china horses, her mouth bloodied and torn, after Kay tells her she has to move out.

Though the film is still oriented around Kay's point of view, a few sequences in this section pointedly mark the limits of her knowledge and her narration. In one example, shot in a straightforward manner, Sweetie, Bob, and Louis go to the beach while Kay is working. When Bob falls asleep, Sweetie approaches Louis, asking him why he and Kay have separate bedrooms. Hearing that it is because Kay has a cold, Sweetie says, "Oh, huh, cold." (Geneviève Lemon's savvy delivery of this line underscores the *other* meaning of cold.) Sweetie then acts to compensate for her sister's "cold" with her own "hot" talents. She asks Louis whether he's ever been "licked all over," telling him she's a "good licker." Louis initially resists her (as he initially resisted Kay), but the scene ends with her jumping on top of him, the two making out.

The effects of this infidelity do come back to Kay, but not in the mode of melodrama and betrayal. Rather, Sweetie's actions inspire Louis not to leave Kay or to have sex with Sweetie, but to *imitate* her, to be "a good licker." That night, he licks Kay's feet and legs while she is sleeping; she wakes up, startled and repulsed, nervously rejecting his advances. In these scenes, the film articulates Sweetie's acting out in a familial economy of replacement and exchange. Her offer to Louis presumes that she and Kay are interchangeable. Louis reacts to Sweetie's acting out by imitating her, thereby becoming insinuated in this economy as *her* replacement. In effect, then, Sweetie licks Kay, the film's plot, as we soon see, imitating the logic of incestuous displacements articulated by Sweetie's actions—one sister for the (m)other.

The second example involves Kay and Sweetie's father Gordon who comes to live with Kay after their mother Flo leaves him. Though Gordon has trouble with Sweetie, he is completely in denial about her mental illness and her lack of talent. He defends her to Kay and Louis, saying, "People like you two don't appreciate it, but the show world is full of unusual types. What's to say Sweetie's any more unusual. She's talented. Jeez, she was a talented little thing—sing, dance, tap." The film flashes back from his perspective to a quick montage of images accompanied by the tinkling of a music box reminiscent of that in *A Girl's Own Story*. We see hands clapping, a girl's feet in ballet shoes, a young Sweetie dancing in her underwear and jumping into her father's arms as a little dog barks viciously at his feet. The rapid cutting together with the dog's extreme agitation complicate the import of this "memory" by infusing the sequence with menace. In these instances, the film's narration exceeds that of Kay, presenting a fragmented reality and consciousness to which she does not have access.

Throughout this part of the film, the only music we hear are one or two instances of diegetic rock and roll, the music box tune, and the ominous tones that initially introduced Sweetie. We hear those tones again when, from Kay's point of view, we see Sweetie bathe her father, playing a game where she drops the soap and perhaps fondles his genitals. In the next shot, we see Kay, in bed, the covers pulled up to her face. The camera pans slowly from her to a close-up of her broken china horses, her mementos from childhood ravaged by Sweetie. Sue Gillett writes of this kind of framing, "This insistence on parts of objects and bodies, on uncentered character placement, on a kind of consciousness given to objects, makes a way for the unconscious to inhabit the film, to be evoked by the film and to be touched, brought to, and taken from the film" ("More Than Meets the Eye," 3).[22] The bathtub scene, with Gordon passive and infantalized, Sweetie active, seductive, and maternal, testifies to a past which cannot be known, but whose perverse effects are everywhere visible and "acted out."

The deteriorating situation at Kay's house is interrupted when Flo calls, inviting Louis and Kay to come visit her in the outback. When they do, they take Gordon with them, who tricks Sweetie so they can leave her behind. If Kay's phobic thoughts begin and dominate the first part of the film and Sweetie's appearance and actions the second, Flo's invitation instigates the final third. As the three set out on their road trip, music plays on the radio as their car moves through expansive landscapes (mountains, desert), getting farther and farther away from the city, small dark rooms, and Sweetie. This part of the film initially focuses on the mother and on the reconstruction of the parental couple. Continuing with distinct uses of music in each section, this last part of the film emphasizes live singing and dancing to a very specific purpose—characterizing Flo's place in this family from which she has been absent until this point. Significantly, the narrative emphasizes the mother's expert performance of the very talents that Gordon has imputed to his daughter Sweetie, talents that have been kept secret. The very first night, as Kay and Louis prepare for bed, they hear Flo singing: "There's a love that waits for you and a love that waits for me." Kay says, shocked, "That's my mother. I've never heard her sing before." Louis voices what we can hear—that she is "quite good."

Later, after a day of swimming and other activities at the ranch, there is a dance under the stars, accompanied by a portable tape player. As Kay and Flo are the only women available, the men left over pair off—in a surreal flourish perhaps inspired by David Lynch, a normal sized jackaroo dances with a dwarf. Kay has several enthusiastic but inept partners, as Louis, in a reversal of their positions, sits petulantly off to the side and refuses to dance or participate in any way. Gordon reappears and cuts in on the jackaroo dancing awkwardly with Flo. Flo and Gordon spin off, moving together with a grace and ease noticeably lacking in any of the other dancers. The next morning Kay finds Flo and Gordon holding hands and smiling, clearly reconciled and ready to go home. On the trip back, Flo, Gordon, Kay, and Louis all sing "There's a love that waits for you" in the car. Their jovial sing-along is suddenly interrupted by a groan and sob from Gordon, who is traumatized by their plans to put Sweetie in a home when they return.

The openness and expanse of the outback sequences are largely rendered in long or medium shots, the camera registering from primarily objective and often distant framings Gordon and Flo's reconciliation and Kay and Louis's increasing alienation from one another. Throughout, there is an emphasis on live diegetic music and performance, the spontaneous, communal singing and dancing we see pointedly oriented around Flo. If the bathtub scene with Sweetie and Gordon depicted a perverse inversion of their proper roles, in this final section the film locates the familial dysfunction in a mother–daughter replacement and exchange that has to do with talent and recognition. Despite Gordon's fantasies, fantasies with which Sweetie is infected, the film reveals that it is Flo, not Sweetie, who can really sing and dance and who is Gordon's more natural (dance) partner.

Once Gordon and Flo are reunited as a result of Flo's asserting her independence and her talents, the rest of the family falls apart. Upon the group's return, Louis leaves Kay, telling her she's "abnormal" after he finds the dead elder tree under her bed. Sweetie goes on a rampage, taking up residence in her "palace in the branches," stark naked with black paint smeared all over her body. From her treehouse, she screams obscenities at the neighbors, farts in her father's face as he climbs a ladder to get her, lures Kay's five-year-old neighbor, Clayton, up the tree with her, and starts jumping wildly up and down. Below, Gordon, Flo, and Kay try to climb up to get her or to rescue Clayton. As the camera focuses on Kay trying to uncoil a garden hose, we hear a crack and crash as the tree house collapses, leaving Sweetie lying on top of the rubble. Flo helps Gordon get up while admonishing Sweetie for her foolishness. Sweetie doesn't move, just turns her head a fraction, and says, "Dad," blood spilling out of her mouth. Kay rushes to help her as her parents stand by, frozen, not even moving when Kay screams at them to call someone. Now both sisters' mouths are bloody as Kay gives her sister artificial respiration, yelling frantically, "Breathe, Sweetie, breathe!" As Sweetie dies in her sister's arms, the camera cuts to Clayton, watching and breathing as hard as he can, and then to the leaves of the tree overhead, shivering in the wind.

Two codas end the film. The first reinstates Kay's voiceover narration and matches the opening of the film. She describes how Sweetie's coffin couldn't even be lowered into the ground because of a tree root that had to be sawed off as we see in long shot the grave and a bulldozer shoveling dirt into it. We again hear the gospel choir and the lyric, "Love will never, never, never let you fall," its meaning now rendered ironic by the circumstances of Sweetie's death. In another long shot, we see Kay opening the door to her house from the end of the hallway. The camera cuts to an overhead angle, mimicking the opening shot of the film, but now instead of two feet below, we see four; instead of the floral carpet, Louis and Kay's feet are side by side in bed, fondling each other as the chorus intones, "Love." They exchange lines of intimate dialogue, as Kay's story ends with her reunited with Louis. This sequence resolves the narrative with one of the standard tropes of industry cinema, couple (re-)formation—Louis and Kay now mirroring the reconstructed parental couple, Gordon and Flo.

The second coda indicates what exists not only outside of narrator Kay's consciousness and control, but also outside of cultural narration generally. Gordon wanders in his backyard, past the wreckage of the treehouse. He turns and looks under the tree, where we see young Sweetie, standing by a picket fence in a pink frilly dress, singing (badly and off key) "With every beat of my heart."

With her white gloves, she pantomimes the beating of her heart and points to her watch to signify "every moment, every hour" she will love the recipient of her song. Sweetie couldn't sing or perform for anyone but her father. Her song ends the film and marks what exceeds its representation and narrative resolution.

Of all Campion's feature films, *Sweetie* has the most noticeably stylized narration, one registered in the film's insistent transgressions of industry cinema's continuity conventions and invisible style.[23] Its eccentric framings often exclude the most important narrative action; its sequence transitions often contain no exposition or continuity information; and the narrative employs very elliptical and arcane plotting, characterization, and dialogue. These elements combine to present the film's narrative as less a hermeneutic chain of cause and effect culminating in coherent resolution and closure than a puzzle from which some of the pieces have been permanently lost. As Sue Gillett astutely notes, the film "generates an apprehension, a re-membering of traumatic response, very much through and not in spite of, the lack of a scene" ("More than Meets the Eye" 6). Rather than engaging us in the plot, in "what happens next," *Sweetie*'s narration provokes us to wonder, "What really happened in this family?" We are left to follow Carlo Ginzburg's

Sweetie singing to her father |

adage: "When causes cannot be reproduced, there is nothing to do but to deduce them from their effects" (117). Campion thwarts our desire for full narrative and moral resolution by limiting the narration's access to the past, thereby emulating the structure of traumatized consciousness. She renders this consciousness as intersubjectively split through the complex structure of the film's narration.

Sweetie's narration stays almost exclusively with Kay, her focus moving from her own inner world to her external view of her sister and then to her mother's new life and her parent's reconciliation. Thus its "analysis" of Kay and her family romance ends, predictably enough, with the mother, but rather than figuring her as the cause of all that has transpired, the film locates her outside of the pathological triangle formed by Kay, Sweetie, and Gordon. Significantly, in selecting Kay to be the film's narrator, Campion has her tell a story that she does not fully know. As the film's title indicates, that story is actually her sister's story, but Sweetie does not have the wherewithal to tell it—instead she acts (it) out against Kay and, through this displacement, it thereby becomes Kay's story to tell. The one who speaks does not know; the one who knows cannot speak. *Sweetie* considers in much greater depth than *A Girl's*

Own Story how the enmity between sisters derives from a trauma to which both are differently subject. The two sisters are doubles for each other (notably, we do not know which is older), their relation allowing Campion to portray the differing effects of that trauma on their sexuality, choices or lack thereof, and character styles.

If the father's memory and questionable valuation of Sweetie's talent ends the film, Kay's ending gives it some semblance of narrative structure and coherence. That coherence derives less from a compelling series of events, which as events appear rather desultory and somewhat banal, than from the displacement of effects—from magical thinking to acting out to inappropriate imitations and exchanges—that motivates the individual characters. Trees recur as visual motif, as crucial plot elements, and as specters that haunt Kay's imaginary, threaten her relationship with Louis, and kill Sweetie. Introduced by but not subsumed within Kay's narration, the trees in *Sweetie* indicate the character of the film's narration—surreal, associative, dispersed, and enigmatic. Through their recurrence, the film articulates a matrix of objective and affective detail thrown into relief by the meta-narrational commentary that keeps the overall tone distanced, dark but comic, devoid of melodramatic judgment or *ressentiment*.

An Angel at My Table: Making Oneself a "First Person"

> [W]ith the autobiographies it was the desire really to make myself a first person. For many years I was a third person—as children are.
>
> —Janet Frame

> Many people haven't suffered to the degree that [Frame] has, and I found it very liberating. There is always something that has attracted me to telling anti-hero stories, and seeing the heroic aspects of them. I'm a lover of the perverse.
>
> —Jane Campion

Jane Campion's second theatrically released feature, *An Angel at My Table* (1990), actually began as a three-part miniseries for New Zealand television that adapted famed New Zealand writer Janet Frame's three-volume *An Autobiography*. Frame wrote her autobiographies to make herself "a first person," one who could narrate her own life and transcend the "third person" she had been as a child and as an "oppressed minority," a woman categorized and incarcerated as mentally ill (Alley 10). Campion knew Frame's work well, having read her novels as a teenager and the autobiography during her years in film school.[24] She actively pursued the adaptation while she was still a film student, saying in interviews that Frame's life could have been her own (Wexman, *Interviews*, 74). Though born thirty years apart and into very different class backgrounds, Campion and Frame nevertheless shared New Zealand childhoods steeped in the arts, emphasized from a nationalist perspective. Frame's career actually was roughly contemporaneous with that of Campion's parents; at the same time they were attempting to establish a national theater, she was beginning to publish and to acquire her reputation as a preeminent New Zealand writer. Thus her autobiographies, their setting, time, and subject, bridged Campion's own creative development and that of her parents.

As she had made *Angel* for television and had crafted its style and approach for the small screen, Campion had to be persuaded to release it as a theatrical feature. Multiple awards at the Sydney and Venice Film Festivals convinced her. Critically very well received, the film made almost twice as much money as it cost to produce.[25] Reviewers noted the Campion touch, finding it "instantly recognizable" as her work (Wexman, *Interviews*, 59). Thus, if the overlap in Frame's and Campion's autobiographies animated the project, Campion's "portrait of the artist" becoming a "first person" enacted her own becoming a "first person," a recognizable artist in international cinema with a distinctive vision and aesthetic sensibility.

The specifics of Frame's autobiography also returned Campion to subjects she had mastered in her student films—unsentimental representations of childhood and adolescence beset by trauma. Janet Frame, one of four sisters, two of whom tragically drowned when they were young, and an epileptic brother, came from a family whose debilitating poverty and tragic losses were somewhat offset for Janet by the family's intense interest and involvement in literature and the arts. The complexity in *Angel* derives from its autobiographical format and the disjunctions in knowledge and time necessarily structured between Janet Frame as the object of the narration (protagonist/character) and as its ostensible subject (narrator).

The film begins with a series of very brief shots that flash on the screen, depicting fragmentary, sensual images from Frame's earliest memories: mother, her arms outstretched, cooing; a baby crawling, walking through grass. The series ends with a long take in which a three- or four-year-old girl (Alexia Koegh) with bright red curly hair walks from the background to the foreground of the image, on a dirt road bordered with bright green fields. Initially positioned above the road, the camera swoops down to the girl's level as she walks toward it. She looks directly into the lens as we hear: "This is the story of my life. In August, 1924, I was born Janet Paterson Frame. My twin brother, who was never named, died two weeks later." Turning nervously first to one side, then the other, the girl takes fright and runs back the way she came as the screen goes to black.

Marking the shift from a prose to a film text, the film's visuals precede the narrator's voice, whose words are taken directly from the autobiography. The disjunction between Janet, the child we see before us, and Janet, the adult voice we hear, concretizes the temporal disparity between the present time of the narration and the past time of the life narrative characteristic of prose autobiography. Campion's framing of this shot takes direction from Frame's writing, but also generates meanings in excess of the passage in Frame:

> My most vivid memory is the long, white dusty road outside the swamp, which filled me with terror for I had been warned never to go near it, and the strange unnaturally bright green grass growing around it—and of myself wearing my most treasured possession, a golden velvet dress. I remember a grey day when I stood by the gate and listened to the wind in the telegraph wires. I had my first conscious feeling of an outside sadness . . . I don't think I had yet thought of myself as a person looking out at the world; until then, I felt I *was* the world. In listening to the wind and its sad song, I knew I was listening to a sadness that had no relation to me, which belonged to the world. (13)

Campion visualizes young Janet "looking out at the world" by having the actress look into the camera lens. If this look separates Janet from the world, it also pointedly separates her from the camera's and the spectator's perspective—we are not looking with her, as we would in a point-of-view shot, but rather directly at her, a look that so terrifies her, she runs off. Thus in its opening, the film's narration incorporates the look of the camera, of the adult Janet Frame remembering herself as a child, and of the audience watching the film; it moves down, confronts and scrutinizes little Janet with more than a hint of sadism.

Through Campion's set up of this shot, Frame's remembered terror of the forbidden swamp becomes specifically visual, whereas in the book it is ultimately *aural*, having to do with language and sound. This shot imagines a specifically visual terror, one that is complex and reversible: seeing things one isn't supposed to see, and, even more frightening, being seen, studied, and evaluated by others and oneself. Thus Campion transforms Frame's concerns with language, sound, and hearing, their promises and terrors, to analogous concerns with vision, imagination, seeing and being seen.

In the ensuing film, Campion uses image and soundtrack to convey the differing emphases of the three volumes of the autobiography as Frame experienced these three different parts of her life. Part One, "To the Is-land," renders Frame's life with her family, the drowning of her older sister, interspersed with her experience at school and with

Young Janet looks at the camera in
An Angel at My Table

friends. In Part Two, "An Angel at My Table," Janet leaves home and the film details her increasingly more harrowing encounters with various public institutions—the university, the primary school where she teaches, the hospital, psychiatric ward, and mental hospital. A younger sister drowns, and Janet experiences debilitating depression. After eight years in a mental institution, she is released when her first book wins a literary prize. When her second book is accepted for publication, she applies for an artist's grant so she can expand her horizons. Part Three, "The Envoy from Mirror City," chronicles her travels and experiences in London, Paris, and Ibiza, experiences which include writing, romance, more stays in hospital (where she learns that she had been misdiagnosed with schizophrenia as a young adult), and finally, her return to New Zealand when her father (Kevin J. Wilson) dies.

Campion carefully modulates objective and subjective cinematography and the frequency and character of autobiographical voiceover to render Frame's developing subjectivity and artistic voice through these different parts of her life. The cinematic strategies she employs in Part One emphasize the autobiographical narrator and the spectator's *distance* from little Janet at the same time that that they cultivate a high degree of pathos. As the film progresses through Parts Two and Three, its narration and, consequently, our spectator position, gets closer and closer to Janet and her internal feelings and perspective. At the same time that the frequency and intimacy of the point-of-view shots increase through the film, the mode of the voiceovers shift as well. Although all of the voiceovers derive from Frame's work, in Parts One and Two they derive exclusively from the autobiography. In Part Three, the quotes from the autobiography are joined by one from Frame's fiction as her thoughts become a writer's thoughts and concerns.

Envisioning the mental life and memory of a child, Part One unfurls in a series of fragments. Its title, "To the Is-land," refers to a pronunciation mistake that Frame once made as a child, and then adopted as an adult to capture the sense of the destination of one's childhood and young adult life: to move toward the being of adulthood by finding a place for oneself (Gillett, "Angel," 7). Accordingly, Campion's challenge in the first section of the film was to represent the experiences and emotion of a child and young adult distinct from the first person narrating and remembering her past life. To effect this distinction for spectators,

Angel's narration provokes our sympathy for young Janet while generally keeping our view distant or distinct from hers. As signaled by the film's opening, Campion develops this distinction within a complex visual economy predicated on the pleasures and dangers of seeing and being seen, articulated from both distanced and progressively more intimate vantage points.

Two similar sequences from the first and second parts of the film illustrate this strategy. In Part One, Janet steals money from her father and distributes gum to all her classmates in an effort to make friends. In the book, this event illustrates how she learned to use words to deceive. Caught by her teacher, Miss Botting (Brenda Kendall), she lies ("my father gave me the money") and acquires the title of "thief" when Miss Botting "gave the news to the class" (26), but her classmates do not witness her confession. Campion's version highlights Miss Botting's fierce gaze at and public interrogation of Janet, which she renders in a tight close-up of Botting. Janet is humiliated visually, forced to stand facing the blackboard through morning class and recess. Finally, she publicly confesses, and then is stared at and called "thief" as she walks to a desk in the back of the room. Though we get close-ups of her suffering at the board, Campion does not give us her point of view throughout this incident.

In an analogous sequence in Part Two, Janet (Kerri Fox) has become an imaginative apprentice grade school teacher, and a school examiner comes to observe her teaching. We see Janet, frozen and terrified by his gaze, against the blackboard, facing him and her class, and then turning to the board, the framing initially identical to when she was punished as a child in Miss Botting's class. But here the filming becomes subjective, as the camera cuts to a close-up of Janet, staring at a piece of chalk, and then to a tight close-up of the chalk from her point of view. The shot, the action, like Janet, freezes. Nervous, the examiner clears his throat. In the cutting back and forth between the students watching her and getting restless, the examiner watching (all in medium or long shot), and close-ups of Janet and shots from her point of view, we shift back and forth between seeing and being seen, objective and subjective perspectives, now closely aligned and identifying with her shame. Janet then excuses herself and flees the school, never to teach again.

In repeated, harrowing instances where Frame is the object of a hostile, public gaze, Campion emphasizes Frame's lifelong, but more abstractly articulated, obsession with how others perceived her and how those perceptions affected her sense of her own identity. Sue Gillett astutely observes that Frame's intense interest in the outside world led her to scrutinize not only herself and how others regarded her, but also "the power of this view from the other." Gillett then argues that Campion's adaptation articulates Frame's point of view by creating spectatorial empathy for Frame through "compassionate, intimate framing" ("Angel," 5). Although Gillett's analysis of Frame's text gets at the ambivalence and complexity of the author's own self-regard, her assertion of Campion's "compassionate framing" does not do justice to the film's complex narration of the powerful view of the other. Some shots do indeed position us close to and in "intimate framing" with Janet, but just as often the camera pins her or others, frequently immobilized and suffering, as its (and our) sadistic point of focus. These shots are particularly prevalent in rendering Janet's childhood. They taper off as she matures as a writer, their sadism thereby associated with Janet's lack of first person-ness.

In Part One, we watch Janet in long shot, centered in a room lined with other children, getting her ears examined and being interrogated about when she last washed. The teacher examining Janet's ears declares to another with disgust, "Filthy." When Janet and her best friend Poppy (Carla Hedgeman) are forbidden to see each other again, Campion also films their good-bye in long shot, the camera perpendicular to the two, who sit centered in the frame. In another, more complex example, we see Janet, in medium long shot, walking alone along the wall of the schoolyard, isolated from all the activity around her, carefully avoiding her epileptic brother, Bruddie (Mark Morrison), only then to watch him, from across the schoolyard, as his schoolmates torment him. Janet here is both agent and recipient of a shaming, isolating gaze. The sequence serves to underscore the class isolation and shame she experienced as a child, occasioned by her family's poverty (her shabby clothes, sporadic hygiene) and her brother's illness, while it also depicts her complicity with that shaming gaze. Set within an autobiographical narration, this moment underscores her retrospective awareness of this complicity.

In these "sadistic" framings that render young Janet's individual and familial isolation, the audience is also positioned as complicit, our view-

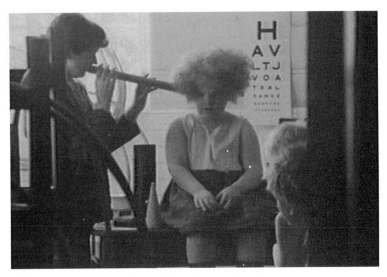

Janet getting her ears examined in
An Angel at My Table

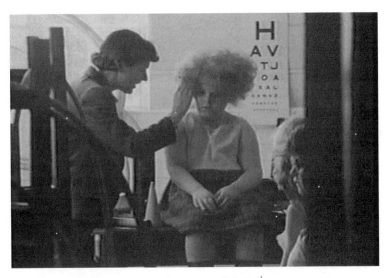

The teacher declares Janet's ears "filthy"

ing position embodying the pressure of others' gazes, others' detached scrutiny. Yet the brilliance of these framings, typically in long shot, is that their very distance, their objectivity, their sadism, operates—like any sadomasochistic relationship—according to a principle of reversibility (Freud 32–35, 58–59). These shots perversely spur our sympathy for little Janet (or her brother or Poppy) as the hapless object of such an isolating look while they also maintain our distance from them. Significantly, the times we share young Janet's point of view are either in traumatic moments (looking at the "crazy" man outside the train, watching her brother have an epileptic fit on the playground) or when that viewpoint is shared with her siblings. These shots emphasize Janet as inhabiting the "third person" of childhood and materialize the great distance that separates her, not only from the spectator, but also from her adult self, the "first person" narrator of the film.

Campion employs several distinct framing patterns to distinguish the different worlds that Frame inhabited (public/private), her very different orientation within these worlds (intimate, alienated, traumatized), and, lastly, our perspective on them. For example, throughout the film, in intimate spaces such as Frame's home, outdoors or in the forest, or in the adult Frame's apartment in Ibiza, the camera travels freely, moving in arcs or curves along with the action, frequently cocooning the space. Multiple camera positions also render the dramatic action from different angles, from the side, and even overhead (as when we see the Frame sisters as children doing the "turn" game in their bed; when Janet, first home from university, tells her sisters about the dashing lecturer, Mr. Forrester; and, much later, in Ibiza, when she swims nude in the Mediterranean with her lover). Outside of what Janet regarded as safe places, however, distanced, perpendicular framings bisect the space, either in proscenium compositions or in those that isolate the characters directly in front of the camera. These latter set-ups clearly locate our perspective outside of the dramatic action which we observe from a distance.

As Janet moves into adolescence, signaled by the change from actress Alexia Keogh to Karen Fergusson, Campion begins to use more intimate point-of-view shots from her perspective. Whereas young Janet's viewpoint was usually established through the use of a medium or long shot, now close-ups capture her wistful gaze at attractive girls at her high school, or later, at couples flirting in a college classroom. Campion spatializes the import of Janet's look, staging each incident such that Janet is physically lower (on a staircase, for example) than those who are the object of her gaze. Thus she literally looks up to them, judging herself by, comparing herself to, a vision of what she is not. Whereas the first part of the film generated young Janet's vulnerability through others' gazes at her, here it constructs adolescent Janet's judgmental view of herself through her envious looks at others, thereby conveying her increasing abjection in relation to her femininity and sexuality. The film thereby progresses through an increasing internalization of sadistic looking, Janet here its object and its agent.

But not all the gazes in the film are negative or hostile. In Part One, a number of proscenium shots render little Janet or others as a positive point of focus: Janet, as "teacher's pet," reciting her poem with Mr. Dymock (Timothy Bartlett) in front of the class; Elizabeth, performing her Spanish dance for the Frame sisters; various children trying out for an acting job on stage, their classmates applauding wildly at their efforts; Janet, taking turns with her sisters and her friends, posturing and walking like models down the length of a tree trunk, while the others applaud and evaluate their poise. In one very special example, Campion underscores the alignment of her own autobiography with Frame's, casting her mother, Edith Campion, to play Janet's teacher, Miss Lindsey, who recites Tennyson's *Idylls of the King* so passionately that Janet "sees" the arm reaching up and grasping hold of jeweled Excalibur.[26] These scenes collectively register young Janet's participation in another visual economy of seeing and being seen—that of imaginative performance and its appreciation. Here Janet is both a successful producer and appreciative audience of an array of skills that include poetry and its recitation, theater, dance, and gender performance, the latter of which will elude her completely when in a heterosexual context.[27] Significantly, these type of performative framings completely disappear in Parts Two and Three, serving primarily to represent young Janet's immersion in a world of creative imagination that she will internalize as an adult. Thus the film itself stages or performs Janet's development and her internalization of both shame and of imaginative production.

Coordinating these different visual framings with the use of voiceover, Campion marks a progression through all three parts whereby Janet, initially the narrated object of the autobiography, comes closer and closer to Janet the narrator until they merge at the last moment rendered by the film. Although the three actresses who represent Frame as a child, as an adolescent, and as an adult all make their appearance in Part One, this section initially compromises our access to Janet's subjective inner world. Almost all of Janet's involvement with literature and poetry in Part One is rendered by external, frequently public, speech. Janet reads out loud to her siblings, and though she writes poetry, we only hear it out loud when she composes it and recites it with Mr. Dymack in class. She publishes her poems, but we only hear the newspaper editor's response, not the poems themselves, when Janet reads it out loud on the hill. While keeping us distant from her, this strategy also complements the scenes of Janet's public shaming with these instances of her public visibility due to her creative talents.

Only three brief instances of voiceover narration convey Janet's thoughts in Part One, one for each of the actresses that plays Janet. The opening voiceover, discussed above, positions young Janet (Alexia Keogh) as the object of an adult narrator. In the second, adolescent Janet (Karen Fergusson), her back to the camera, writes to her imaginary confidant of the tears she shed reading "The Scholar Gypsy," and that she has "made up her mind" to forgo teaching and become a poet. The film withholds our view of her face as we listen to Janet narrating thoughts about herself. Toward the end of Part One, in the shot that introduces actress Kerry Fox, the adult Janet, her back to the camera, walks along railroad tracks with a book held out in front of her as she reads one of Frame's favorite passages: "Life is sweet, Jasper, there's day and night, Jasper, both sweet things."[28] Here, the voiceover narrates Frame's imaginative inner life, bringing us closer to her, while the visuals depict her imagination in relation to her increasing alienation from the world around her. Shortly after this scene, Janet leaves to attend the university, and Part One ends.

Campion marks Frame's progress toward becoming a first person through the occurrence of voiceover narration which increases dramatically in Parts Two and Three.[29] But the character of the voiceover in each section is very different. In Part Two, the voiceovers serve to bring us closer to Frame the narrator as well as to Frame the traumatized autobiographical subject, while also keeping narrator and narrated temporally distinct through the use of verb tense. At the same time that the voiceovers bring us closer to Frame, the visuals depict her increasing isolation from everyone. We see her either alone (in a graveyard, reading, writing, and disposing of her menstrual rags; in a park, walking, sobbing; in her aunt's kitchen, surreptitiously wolfing down scraps of food) or isolated and silent in shots filled with other people laughing and talking in university classrooms and hallways. In Part Two, Janet is never really at home; her own body, her femininity, and her physical needs are onerous and overwhelming to her.[30] Overall, the camera set-ups are more conventional; rather than bisecting the dramatic space at a remove from the action, the camera generally moves or cuts to different perspectives within it. We get many more shots from Janet's point of view, depicting how interaction with others becomes increasingly difficult for her. Accompanying these visuals, voiceovers communicate Janet's private thoughts to us, usually conveying a collective or generalized sense of past events. As she sits alone in a deserted biology lab, book open in her lap, eating her lunch, she stares into space (at a slight angle from the camera), and we hear, "Too shy to mix, too scared to enter the union building, I was more and more alone. My only romance was in poetry and literature."

When Janet's sister Isabel (Glynis Angell), in a tragic repetition, drowns, the incident sends Janet into a terrible depression. Misdiagnosed with schizophrenia, Frame is institutionalized and subjected to a "new experimental treatment"—electroshock therapy. As Frame writes only very briefly of this period in *An Autobiography*, Campion uses Frame's novel about a woman in a mental institution, *Faces in the Water*, to depict it (Henke 652). To evoke the strongest possible contrast with Frame's life outside of mental institutions, Campion shifts from the warm palette she has used prior to this point and neutralizes the colors in the mise-en-scène, keeping everything bluish white. Crowds of inmates moan and flail in front of the camera, the blocking of these scenes depicting an anonymous, despairing chaos, interspersed with Frame's horrified looks, and later, her shuffling, zombie-like walk down a corridor after years of electroshock. To signal the compression Frame uses to render these years, only one voiceover accompanies these sequences, tersely summarizing her experience: "Over the next eight years, I received more than two hundred applications of electroshock treatments, each one equivalent in fear to an execution." It is her writing—her "only romance" and her "comfort"—that saves her. Frame's first book is published and wins a prize, sparing her from having a lobotomy and further incarceration. She takes up residence in a small cottage adjacent to that of another writer, Frank Sargeson (Martyn Sanderson), writes her first novel, and, encouraged by Frank and an artist's grant she receives, takes off for Europe as Part Two ends.

In Part Three, "The Envoy from Mirror City," Frame moves through foreign cities and settings, still alone, but now much more the agent rather than the hapless object of the narration. The word "schizophrenia," with which she had been labeled, is proven false. Rather than conveying in general retrospective terms her inner state over a period of time, as in Part Two, the voiceover narration now clearly articulates her own responses to events as we see them happening on screen. Coming home one day to find another lodger in her residence, Frame meets him as we hear, "I felt sick with disappointment and a sense of betrayal, for I had believed I had rented the entire house." Though still in the past tense, the alignment of narration and event is specific and concrete. Depicting her process, not of becoming a writer (for she publishes her first book of short stories and her novel in Part Two), but of becoming a person who can tell and write her own story, *An Angel at My Table* ends with Janet writing as we see and hear (in voiceover) what she is writing as she writes it. In this, the autobiographical present, Frame the narrator and Frame the narrated become one. Whereas Frame ends her autobiography with a meditation on the artist's role as an envoy from the mirror city of the imagination, Campion ends the film with an event that happens several chapters earlier when Frame writes her first autobiographical essay in the caravan behind her sister's house.

In adapting Frame's *An Autobiography*, Campion not only remained "faithful" to the traumatic events of Frame's life, but also set herself the tasks of cinematically representing Frame's psychic development, the internalization of her shame and creativity, and the imaginative process whereby Frame became the narrator of her own life. Campion also certainly intends the implicit pun on her subject's name in the conversion of her story to cinema, her film consistently exploring, visually, aurally, and narratively, all the ways Janet Frame was framed by others and, perhaps even more significantly, by herself. When Frame first learned to spell,

The autobiographical present in
An Angel at My Table

three words stood out—"decide, destination, and observation"—all three of which Frame related to "adventure" (35). *Angel* takes these up as key words, for example, distributing its emphasis on the different positions implicit in *observation* through the film's three sections: first, being observed; second, observing oneself; and third, becoming an artist, an observer who synthesizes perspectives of the world and the imagination. Campion charted these transformations through the changing character of the voiceovers and increased uses of subjective cinematography from section to section. Similarly, travel and different destinations frame each section. Part One begins and ends with a train trip, the train defining, cutting across the horizon(tal) of the image; Part Two ends and Part Three begins with the wake of a ship vertically dividing the image. Part Three ends, significantly, with a stationary travel caravan, parked in back of Janet's sister's house, with Janet, the envoy from mirror city, typing, writing, traveling to and from our world and that of her imagination. After completing this film, Campion turned to a creative project that she had first envisioned while she was in film school, a project that became *The Piano.*

The Piano: Surrealism, Melodrama, and Mimetic Infection

The opening shot of *The Piano* presents us with a dense and initially indecipherable visual pun. First we see slanted slats of light with rose- and flesh-colored margins that we only retrospectively grasp as protagonist Ada McGrath's point of view—the reverse angle depicts her looking through her fingers with her hands in front of her face. Over this second shot, we hear her voiceover: "The voice you hear is not my speaking voice but my mind's voice. I have not spoken since I was six years old. No one knows why, not even me. My father says it is a dark talent and the day I take it into my head to stop breathing will be my last." These two opening shots establish our identification with narrator/protagonist Ada by way of provocative enigmas in the image (an inscrutable then tactile point-of-view shot) and sound (if what we are hearing is not spoken but imagined, we are inside Ada's head, being addressed both inter- and intrasubjectively).[31] Indeed, an analogous enigma underwrites Ada's own self-representation and will—she does not speak and does not know why.[32]She is therefore not fully present to herself.

Mute by will, if not by choice,[33] Ada communicates through script, sign, gesture, and, most importantly for her, by the playing of her piano. As signaled by the opening shot, her fingers constitute her perspective and her "voice." The alignment of her gaze and ours with her fingers constitute only the first of the many narrative concerns emanating from this visual pun—digits. Digits are fingers, numbers, and, in the adjectival form, any key played with a finger, as on a piano. As agents of communication, aesthetic expression, and accounting, *The Piano*'s digits figure in the pointedly interrelated modes of exchange—semiotic, aesthetic, economic—insistently invoked in this narrative that explores the patriarchal exchange of women in relation to colonialist enterprise.[34]

We hear this connection explicitly articulated as Ada's opening voiceover continues: "Today [my father] married me to a man I've not yet met. Soon my daughter and I shall join him in *his own* country" (emphasis mine). It is hard to miss both the emphatic (and gendered) redundancy and irony of "his own country," for Stewart, the man Ada's father has contracted to marry her, is Scottish, as is she, yet "his own country" is the colony, identified here as his possession, New Zealand. Ada's statement simultaneously positions her as an object of exchange (between her father and Stewart) and as a subject possessed of a colonial imaginary (she voices Stewart's proprietary relation to New Zealand). Registering the complex ethical aspirations of the film's narration, this voiceover comments on colonialism and its link to the patriarchal oppression of Western women, but it does so from the imaginary perspective of just such a woman who nevertheless voices, embodies, and perpetuates a proprietary colonial ethos.[35]

Significantly, the film's opening moments situate Ada's predicament and perspective in relation to problems of perception and subjectivity. Though the opening shot constitutes our point of view, we cannot see or understand it as such, save retrospectively, from the reverse angle, from the point of view of the other. Similarly, Ada's initial address to us on the soundtrack asserts an inextricable confounding of what is between two subjects (speaker and spoken to), and what is within one (hearing her mind's voice, we are in her head). It is a stunning opening conceit in a film whose narrative consistently confounds encounters between genders, generations, nations, and races with narrational strategies that blur or confuse subjective boundaries (between characters; between character and audience).

Although Campion has routinely been criticized for *The Piano*'s depiction of the Maori and colonialism (Dyson, Neill, Orr, Pihama, Reid, Simmons), such critiques do not fully register Ada's ethical positioning (ironic from the outset), or the narrative complexity derived from the range of associations the film brings to bear on her tale.[36] In this sense, an autoethnographic impulse motivates the film: Campion wanted to tell a story about *her* "strange heritage as a *pakeha* New Zealander" descended from English colonizers like "Ada and Stewart and Baines" (Bilborough 135).[37] But what is key is that Campion pursues this impulse not only through the anthropological, but also through surrealism, literature, and art in a way that complicates the treatment of colonialism. In the narrative, Ada arrives on a desolate New Zealand beach with her daughter Flora (Anna Paquin) and her most prized possession, her piano, to meet husband Stewart, who then refuses to carry it to his home inland. Instead he trades the piano for land owned by his employee, Baines, who then proposes a highly exploitive exchange to Ada: sexual favors for piano keys so she can repossess her own property, her own voice. Yet in their exchange, Baines loses his heart, and, wanting Ada to care for him, gives her piano back to her. His gift, his giving up, compels Ada to give in and she falls in love with him; Stewart then finishes off the series of exchanges, possessions, and reversals with a final, horrific exchange—Ada's index finger for the piano key she has sent to Baines. Ada, Flora, and Baines leave Stewart in the brush, and as they disembark, Ada goes overboard with her piano, then swims to the surface, her will choosing life. The three settle in the metropole, Nelson; the film ends on Ada's fantasy, her lullaby, of being tethered to her submerged piano resting on the ocean floor.

To render her diverse heritage within this narrative, Campion drew heavily from its imaginary and archival residue, blending nineteenth-century sources with those taken from her own life and work experience. Her literary and aesthetic inspirations included nineteenth-century British fiction by women (the Brontës, especially Emily); American poetry (Emily Dickinson); and twentieth-century Mexican surrealist art (Frida Kahlo). *Wuthering Heights* was particularly influential. A part of Campion's own imaginative development, the novel also was of the moment she wished to represent, having been written and published during the late 1840s. Set in 1850, the film depicts contemporaneous New Zealand in the period of its most intensive colonial settlement (Wexman, *Interviews*, 99–100, 114–15). Similarly, in imagining Ada, Campion devised a composite of the women artists who inspired her, giving her character Emily Brontë's silence, Emily Dickinson's secrecy, and Frida Kahlo's fierce gaze (110, 115).[38] Thus the colonial female narrator of *The Piano* embodies a complex transnational and transhistorical feminine imaginary self-consciously derived from Campion's individual, familial, professional, and *pakeha* heritage.

Complementing her animation of this romantic and surreal imaginary were material and approaches Campion took from the colonial archive and its intellectual heritage. Significantly, the most active colonization of New Zealand occurred a decade after the development of photography and around the time of anthropology's establishment as an independent discipline (Fabian xi). Campion, using her ethnographic training, appropriated film images from colonial era photographs of *pakeha* settlers and Maoris she had researched in New Zealand's Turnbull Library. The costumes for the film's Maori characters, which combined European clothing with indigenous dress, were taken from these photos, their clothing providing "a graphic metaphor for their understanding of Europeanism" (Wexman, *Interviews,* 114). A colonial image "of a woman whose head appeared between sheets" in amateur theater inspired the Bluebeard production in *The Piano* (102), a reference that also alludes to Campion's parents' careers.

Campion's vision of colonial New Zealand also appears to have taken up and revised her father Richard Campion's utopian thematic and visual concerns with the same period. His production design for *Green are the Islands?* a play he produced that depicted the conflicts between and coming together of Maori and *pakeha* cultures, anticipates *The Piano's* mise-en-scène, particularly Stewart's house, with its dead tree stumps, and the Victorian meeting hall.[39] Peter Harcourt described this "highly original" production from the late 1960s as follows:

> To illustrate the coming of the birds to the cool damp forest that covered the land, the New Zealand ballet swooped and darted in specially designed costumes. Following them came scenes of early Maori settlement and community life. Then, into this idyllic setting there blundered huge new shapes bringing strangely-garbed people who cut down the trees, ploughed up the land and turned the country into a frontier imitation of a Victorian provincial town. After a suggestion of the battles between these newcomers and the displaced Maoris, a rousing finale presented the coming together of all people as New Zealanders. (Harcourt 145)

In addition to revising this story and telling it from a colonial woman's perspective, Campion also withholds an earlier generation's (her father's) idealistic vision and resolution. Finally, to apprehend the language of her colonial characters, Campion also read travel diaries by women and European settlers, and literature and children's books of the period, an illustration from the latter providing the animated image of Flora's father burning up after having been struck by lightning (Wexman, *Interviews,* 103, 114).

In fashioning a history of her colonial ancestors, Campion envisions a wildly romantic plot and characters knee deep in the mud and thicket of 1850s New Zealand. She herself suggested, and many critics have written insightfully on, the gothic/melodramatic character of this combination of fantasy and realism (Allen, Gorbman, Hardy, Jayamanne,

Orr, Robinson, Thompson). Yet another approach is to speculate on what happens to melodrama fixed with an *ethnographic* gaze. In *The Piano*, an otherworldly heroine, derived from a Western imaginary, encounters a geographic, historical, and ethnographic materiality drawn from the colonial archive, a surreal juxtaposition in which the colonial milieu historicizes the European imaginary rather than vice versa.[40] Upsetting the convention whereby the West represents history to the indigenous other inhabiting a mythic or prehistorical time,[41] the film systematically effects other representational inversions or reversals by way of ironic framings and surreal visual flourishes that comment on otherwise romantic or melodramatic moments.

The nature of that commentary is less didactic than provocative and enigmatic. Speaking of his work on *The Piano*, the director of photography, Stuart Dryburgh, remarked, "The camera's viewpoint [. . .] is that of a witness directing the viewer's attention in a very intimate way. Sometimes we go places where the camera can't really go. We've been inside the piano, inside Stewart's pocket, right down at the level of hands and fingers and teacups. It wouldn't be a Jane Campion film without some wittiness in the framing" (Campion 141). The cinematographer's astute, if perhaps inadvertent, pun, of the witness and wittiness of Campion's camera references two distinct framings that generate ethnographic commentary from their surreal visual wit.

In the first of these, the camera is literally in Stewart's pocket, depicting his fingers reaching in to grasp a small oval photo of Ada that he pulls out to contemplate as he, Baines, and a group of Maori porters make their way to the beach to meet Ada and Flora. The wittiness of the framing also gives witness to Stewart's sense of Ada. Like money, she is in his pocket. He has acquired her in the same way we see him acquiring Baines's land with Ada's piano and the Maoris' land and labor—by contract and exchange. But for Campion, the economics of colonialism and patriarchy are enmeshed with issues of self-representation and identification.

As the sequence continues, we watch Stewart look at Ada's image, then tilt it slightly such that it becomes a mirror he uses to look at himself. This moment bears an uncanny, significantly gender-inverted, resemblance to a famous surrealist photo by Maurice Tabard described by Rosalind Krauss: "[I]n *Hand and Woman* (1929), a looking-glass is explicitly present, a handmirror held by the woman in such a way that it both obliterates her face and seems to call into being the shadowy, threatening, faceless male presence behind her—as though it were his image, on the other side of hers as its obverse, that the mirror reflected" (82). Interestingly, the Tabard photo visually anticipates Laura Mulvey's famous argument about women's cinematic image solely representing male subjectivity and desire. In *The Piano*'s rendering of a gendered gaze, Stewart looks at Ada's photo and therein becomes captivated by his own reflection; as his gaze shifts from contemplating his possession (Ada) to contemplating himself, his narcissistic thrall arrests the Maori workers, Baines, and the narrative itself (as Mulvey argued the woman's body did). Momentarily disconnected from an economy of possession (of Ada, of the Maoris' labor, of himself), Stewart cannot hear Baines's repeated question: "Are we stopping?" Only when all of the Maori porters have sat down does Stewart rouse himself, saying sharply, "We must get on." Even as the scene registers Stewart's narcissistic self-involvement, it also astutely depicts that narcissism as a dispossession, his access to his own image absolutely dependent on its obverse, what he sees himself as possessing (Ada and her image, the Maoris and their labor).

In the second instance, Stewart voices his concerns about Ada (lacking her piano, she has begun to play the table, and he fears she is "brain-affected") to Aunt Morag (Kerry Walker) over tea. Continuing on a more optimistic note, he observes, "And with time, she will, I'm sure, become affectionate," as we see an overhead close-up of the delicate floral tea cup he holds in his large hands as he stirs his tea with a tiny silver spoon. The image appoints his hesitant euphemism ("affection" for "sex") with tea and teacup, a beverage and an object that epitomize the ruse, the front of British empire—its civility. This civility both necessitated the acquisitive brutality of colonialism, its tea plantations, and other mechanisms of procurement, and masked it through the performance of daily civil rituals and carefully arched pinky fingers.[42]

Campion's witty but emphatic framings in these scenes imbricate the fundamental ironies of imperial and patriarchal civility and possession through Stewart and the objects he handles—Victorian photo and teacup. Registering the trappings of modernity and empire, these serve an alternately comic and historical refashioning and contextualizing of film melodrama. As various critics have observed, the genre typically features stories wherein problems with speech or expression are foregrounded, sometimes in characters who are literally mute. Consequently, what is repressed or cannot be spoken registers itself dramatically in the mise-en-scène. As Thomas Elsaesser argues:

> [T]he domestic melodrama in colour and widescreen . . . is perhaps the most highly elaborated, complex mode of cinematic signification the American cinema has ever produced, because of the restricted scope for external action determined by the subject and because everything, as Sirk said, happens 'inside.' [This] sublimation of dramatic conflict into décor, colour, gesture and composition of frame [. . .] in the best melodramas is perfectly thematised in terms of the characters' emotional and psychological predicaments. (52)

The Piano does indeed feature a mute protagonist as well as pointed framings and pronounced visual emphases on various body parts (legs, hands, fingers) and objects (ax, piano, Victorian photo, teacup), thereby mimicking the representational mode of melodrama. But it invests the affective sublimation that conventionally shapes melodramatic mise-en-scène and framing with historical and ethnographic significance.

Similarly, Ada's enigmatic silence does not underscore her weakness or elicit pathos, but rather operates as the source of her power and mystery over Stewart, Baines, and the film's audience, as she is our narrator. The character of her narration and the film's narration overall both solicits and distances our identification, repeatedly engaging us in a dialectic of affective immersion and ironic, frequently amused contemplation. Although the film uses voiceover narration and music (as Ada's voice) to blur distinctions between internal and external, subjective and objective states, thereby merging our perspective with certain characters in an aurally intersubjective space, in contrast, its relentless play with the gaze and mimicry disperses our identification among different sensory registers (visual, tactile) and characters.

In the first instance, the film's musical score systematically exploits the paradoxical relationship between nondiegetic and internal diegetic sound. Nondiegetic sound comes from a source outside the narrative; most film music is nondiegetic and its primary function is to shape and direct the emotional responses (sadness, romance, suspense) of the spectator. As narration, such sound is objective and omniscient, as it is not related to nor limited by any character or their knowledge. Internal diegetic sound, by contrast, is "represented as coming from the mind of a character within the story space" (Bordwell and Thompson 310). Subjective and restricted, this use of sound expresses a character's inner thoughts or feelings. Campion exploits the formal similarity of these otherwise opposing types of sound (each is identified by the fact that it cannot be heard by characters in the story space) to confuse them. As Ada looks down at her piano from a cliff or Baines gazes at it in his house after Ada has left, the source of the piano music we hear is undecidable. Are we hearing, sharing Ada's imagination, Baines' memory or the film's voice, its emotional prompt to its spectators? The piano music, like the exchange of the piano keys for sexual favors, passes back and forth between Ada and Baines, but also "creeps inside" the mind of the spectator, constituting Ada's narrational voice at the level of affect. It thereby immerses us in an ethereal, intersubjective space which dramatizes the slow erotic dissolution of Ada and Baines's sense of self-possession, a countermovement to the fierce struggles for object possession (the piano, the Maori land, Ada) that otherwise dominate the narrative.

This use of music exists in some tension with the film's emphasis on mimicry and mimetic modes of representation, both forms of inter-act-ing and "acting out" within the colonial scene. Not only do characters imitate one another in the moment, as when the Maori mimic and mock Stewart, Baines imitates the Maoris, Nessie (Geneviève Lemon) imitates and echoes Aunt Morag, and Flora imitates Ada, but the film is also littered with examples of characters repeating the actions of others at moments distinct in time. Just as Flora watches her mother and Baines through a hole in Baines's cabin, so too does Stewart. Ada imitates herself kissing Baines by kissing a mirror after she can no longer see him. Nessie jumps back in horror at the shadow play of the Reverend hitting her hand with a cardboard ax just as the Maori spectators for the Bluebeard play rush the stage to save Bluebeard's wife from his attack. In these imitations and simulations, the film mobilizes the mimetic faculty, what Michael Taussig describes as "the two-layered notion of mimesis that involve[s] a copying or imitation, and a palpable, sensuous connection between the very body of the perceiver and the perceived (20–21).[43] It does so within hierarchical relationships between generations, genders, classes, colonizer and colonized, thereby insinuating psychic, developmental, and ethnographic senses of mimicry and the mimetic faculty. Further, as the example of the Bluebeard play indicates, character mimicry is insinuated with the film's repeated, self-reflexive uses of aesthetic mimetic forms—illustrated storytelling, drama, mime, and photography—providing the means whereby the human interactions in the narrative are insistently referred to questions of representation, questions which implicate the film's spectators.

In this respect, *The Piano*'s colonial romance of barter, mimicry, loss, and suffering, conveyed by an ironic synthesis of ethnographic, surreal, and melodramatic modes, marks its historical specificity by pointed uses of photography. It does so to a specific purpose. Stewart's possession of Ada is denoted by his possession of her photo. Lest we miss the point, soon after Ada arrives, she is dressed in tie-on lace that simulates a wedding gown and led out in the rain to pose with Stewart for their wedding photo. After Aunt Morag positions her in front of a banal backdrop, Stewart looks at her through the camera's viewfinder, the cinematic shot capturing his one blue eye looking at her. Again, his eye, his gaze, and their significance are precisely rendered. Aunt Morag has reassured Ada, "If you cannot have a ceremony together, you have at least a photograph." Her words signal a moment where simulation takes precedence over ritual, the visual *object* taking the place of experience and internalized memory. The advent of photographic technology in the nineteenth century heralded a new phase of modernity whose technologies of mechanical reproduction instituted an increasingly pervasive regime of visual representation, enshrining vision and the look as object (the photo) to the detriment of other senses and human faculties (the tactile, the mimetic).

Significantly, the film insists on precisely those faculties in its narration of the incongruities, the incommensurabilities that make up the unequal power relations animating this text. These inequalities become representational rather than moral problems, referenced to mimetic relations rather than melodramatic revelation. The film implements this on four levels, articulating relations of imitation within the hierarchical power relationships of patriarchy, class, generation, and race represented in the film. If ethnography is a way of engaging and schematizing the other, and colonialism and patriarchy are modes of violence against the other, then mimicry, the imitation of the subordinated other, discovers the masochism latent in the first two relations; to imitate one against whom you exert schematic power and violence is to simulate yourself as an object of that violence. Mimicry is thereby crucial to what Gilles Deleuze refers to as the masochistic relation, "a whole technique of dialectical reversal, disguise and reduplication" (22). In repeated instances in *The Piano*, characters with power imitate those who do not have it, these imitations working to subordinate the one to the other. This technique undergirds the affective and economic reversals that occur among the main characters, reversals that also implicate the film's spectators.

Ada and Baines, differently disempowered by gender and class, share disabilities with respect to language and representation (she cannot speak, he cannot write);[44] the film affiliates them at the level of music—she plays, he hears her passion, one that he cannot deflect from the piano to himself until he has utterly succumbed to her loss. He gives up and thereby assumes power over her. She mimics his dispossession, gives in, gives herself up to him. If the film's soundtrack involves us in the multiple reversals of erotic possession and submission between Ada and Baines, it also insinuates us in Flora and Stewart's acts of voyeurism and mimetic infection at the level of the image.

We share Flora's point of view as she watches her mother rub against Baines through a crack in the wall of his cabin. We then see her and her Maori friends exercising their collective mimetic faculties as they kiss and suggestively rub up against trees. Stewart, outraged by Flora's behavior, understands her tree-love from the perspective of a colonial subject rather than a celibate husband; he thinks she is imitating the Maoris, not her mother, his wife. (As with *Sweetie*, this confusion between the other and the mother is an insistent motif in Campion's films). He is wrong but also right, his misreading correctly apprehending the mimetic relation, implemented at the level of the narrative, between patriarchal and colonial systems of oppression.

To punish Flora, Stewart has her whitewash the tree trunks. Through the visual pun of whitewashing, the film contrasts Flora's playful mimicry with Stewart's abstract, moral, and racialized judgment that institutes metaphoric erasure as goodness. This scene, one of many throughout the film, aligns two distinct modes of knowing, the first predicated on sensuous imitation and directed toward pleasure, the second predicated on repression and a self-conscious adherence to social values and discipline. Flora moves from one to the other. Wretched with jealousy at the loss of her mother to Baines, she implicates Stewart in that loss by introducing him to the mystery of Baines's piano lessons: "She never gives him a turn. She just plays whatever she pleases and sometimes she doesn't play at all." She thereby leads Stewart to take up her position as audience, as voyeur to these lessons, as she will then assume the small power of his moralistic, proprietary viewpoint. She assists him when he boards up the house, incarcerating Ada, and admonishes her, "You shouldn't have gone up there [to see Baines]." When she delivers the piano key Ada intended for Baines to Stewart, she tells him that she didn't think it "the proper thing" to carry out her mother's instructions.

Meanwhile Stewart takes up Flora's position as voyeur at the crack in Baines's cabin, and sees what Flora has seen before him: Ada and Baines having sex. He initially turns away, then looks back, as Baines maneuvers himself under Ada's skirts and her head tilts back in pleasure. The camera moves from Stewart's point of view to a position behind him, tilting down to show us a dog licking his hand. This cut—from Stewart watching his wife's expressions of pleasure from an act he cannot see to what he can then feel, simulated, on his hand—has absolutely no narrative motivation. It comes directly to us, the spectators, from the filmmakers themselves, a sly wink, a meta-narrative mimetic joke. Stewart

Stewart looking at Ada being pleasured
by Baines in *The Piano*

responds with stupefaction, blankly rubbing his hand on the outside wall, literally and metaphorically out of touch.

Stewart does not get the connection between what he is not seeing but can imagine (cunnilingus) and what he is experiencing but cannot feel (the dog's tongue). Significantly, we do get it, the dramatic irony evoked in a very particular way. In her somewhat perverse exploration of the cinema's capacity to excite the mimetic faculty, Campion uses Stewart and his hand as the medium for our tactile apprehension of the joke, our pleasure derived from his pain. Thus masculinity and masculine suffering become a diegetic vehicle whereby certain sensations are conveyed to the audience. The positioning of the spectators here is quite complex: we are both identified with Stewart's voyeuristic point of view, even as we have a perspective in excess of it, that excess being precisely tactile and mimetic. This instance of mimetic contagion is implicated both in a scenario of suffering and also in ambiguous relations of power. That is, in the same moment that the film implicates us in the cinema's mimetic power, it also enacts a perverse chain of various kinds of submission in which Stewart is positioned as both master and cuckold. Stewart watches his wife being pleasured by someone who submits to and works for *him*, his voyeuristic position signaling his disempowerment.[45] He does not rush in to stop the act; rather, he crawls *beneath* Baines, *under* Ada, now at the bottom of a hierarchy he began

Stewart beneath Baines, under Ada, in *The Piano*

by dominating, lying below the floor, mesmerized by another kind of dispossession, his own suffering.

The drama that ensues from this scene of masculine suffering occurs within a pointedly self-reflexive frame. When Stewart goes after his diminutive wife with an ax, he mimics the actions of Bluebeard, whose tale he witnessed in shadow play earlier in the film. During that performance, he, Ada, and Baines watched as several Maori men rushed the stage to save Bluebeard's wife from being beheaded with an ax. If this scene initially appears to endorse modernity's inscription of the primitive as those who don't "get" representation or the logic of simulation, Stewart's mimicry radically reverses this apparent endorsement. Though in the moment it seems like a joke about the Maori, retrospectively, we see that they do "get" it; indeed, they do understand something that we do not. Unlike the audience, they are witness to and active in trying to stop the thing that Stewart will ultimately do.

Significantly, we "get" the undoing of the joke in a scene that, as with Stewart and the dog, solicits our tactile, mimetic identification, only now to horrific rather than humorous effect. Recalling perhaps the most shocking use of mimetic identification/infection in the cinema, Luis Buñuel and Salvador Dali's slicing of a woman's eye in extreme close-up in *Un Chien Andalou*, *The Piano* depicts Stewart bringing down his ax on Ada's small, outstretched fingers. Just as Buñuel and Dali graphically severed the very organ connecting their spectators to their film, electrifying them with adrenaline and putting them in an appropriately surrealist state of mind (both vigilant and stunned, paranoid and elated), so Campion does the same, capitalizing on her spectators, tactile and perceptual identification with Ada's fingers, cultivated by the film from the outset. As a result, this moment elicits a powerfully visceral mimetic response. If the narratives of these two films are surprisingly similar—a love triangle that culminates in violence and an enigmatic ending having to do with a frozen moment of immersion (in sand in the former, water in the latter), these sequences that each generate mimetic shock occur in very different moments in the plot of each film—at the beginning of *Un Chien Andalou* and near the end of *The Piano*. Whereas in the former film this moment physically conditions its spectatorship, in the latter the shock to the audience attends the alignment of Stewart with

Bluebeard and the eruption of the heroine's "dark talent," her indomitable and inscrutable will.

Following the dictates of her will, a force that she does not understand and whose workings are a surprise to her, Ada loses a finger. Subsequently, her mind's voice penetrates her husband's consciousness and insists that he let her go with Baines because "I am frightened of my will, of what it might do, it is so strange and strong." Her will compels her to go overboard with her piano as she, Baines, and Flora disembark to Nelson, and it surprisingly chooses life as she struggles out of the rope around her shoe and surfaces. As she surfaces, we again hear Ada's mind's voice: "I teach piano now in Nelson. George has fashioned me a metal fingertip; I am quite the town freak, which satisfies. At night, I think of my piano in its ocean grave, and sometimes of myself floating above it. Down there everything is so still and silent that it lulls me to sleep. It is a weird lullaby and so it is. It is mine." Ada still plays her piano but in place of seamless sonic immersion, its harmonic and complete production, her music is accompanied now by the click, click, click of her metal fingertip against the keys.

Although some critics have suggested that in Ada, Campion had imagined a twentieth-century heroine in a nineteenth-century tale, Ada's most distinctive trait is *not* her modernity but the fact that, as Carol Jacobs has observed, "she is not the locus of decision of mind." Jacobs associates the irrational relation of Ada to her own will with the text's elusive "a-morality" and its "radical politicality" (Jacobs 772). Through Ada, but also through Stewart and Baines, Campion creates her own hypothetical ancestors and, by implication, a genealogy for the present that constitutes what Wendy Brown calls a "perverse mastery" over history. One triumphs "over the past by reducing its power, by remaking the present against the terms of the past—in short, by a project of self-transformation that arrays itself against its own genealogical consciousness" (72). Such a transformation calls for different configurations of power and ethics construed outside of established representational conventions of truth and morality.

Campion effects this transformation by altering the idealistic *pakeha* narrative of her father's generation—one in which two distinct cultures confront one another and then all come together as New Zealanders.

Instead, she tells the story of four colonials—Ada, Stewart, Baines, and Flora—identifying the first three specifically as her ancestors. Ada and Stewart are each self-enthralled (he to his own possessive utility, she to her self-enclosed imaginary) and thereby utterly, though differently, indifferent to their surroundings. Baines, by contrast, is enthralled with the other—first the Maori, then Ada. (Flora, a child, a cipher, shifts from one of these ancestors to the other, subject to the confrontations among them.)[46] Significantly, the Maoris are not indifferent—they rush the stage, interrupt the staged performance of patriarchal violence. They have knowledge of the colonial character to which we are not privy. Significantly, Campion does not presume to tell their story, to speak for them and their experience of colonialism. Her focus is on her ancestors—colonizers whose patriarchal and class relations mimic their colonial subordination of the Maori.

In Ada's tale, Ada acts—she follows her will and her desire—and both her husband and Baines manipulate and punish her with acts of increasingly horrific violence. Yet rather than condemning this violence, framing it as the reprehensible actions of the strong against the weak, or alternately vesting Ada with superhuman strength, Campion forgoes both melodrama and utopia. She does so by replacing rational causality with "irrational" character and narrative motivations: surreal associations and mimetic relations. She is not interested in the pathos of victimization but in the struggle and consequences of engaged conflict between people with unequal access to established forms of power. In the end, the click, click, click of the metal fingertip that mars Ada's once harmonious and intersubjective sound, the drawbacks of Baines as a partner, and the oddity of the narrative's irresolution satisfy precisely because they all lack the ring of truth, the resolute closure of a moral story.

The Portrait of a Lady: From James to Jane

> She would have given her little finger at that moment to feel strongly and simply the impulse to answer: "Lord Warburton, it's impossible for me to do better in this wonderful world, I think, than commit myself, very gratefully, to your loyalty."
>
> —Henry James

Jane Campion's adaptation of Henry James's *The Portrait of a Lady* (1996) begins with a black screen on which we see the opening credits. In voiceover, we hear women from Australia and New Zealand discussing erotic attraction, love, and coupling. When the voices finish, we see a diverse group of fifteen or so contemporary young women in the woods—black, white, Maori, South Asian, mixed race—as the film's fluted musical motif plays. Initially the women, in their teens to early twenties, form a circle, lying on the ground with the camera overhead, making an empty frame in which the text "A film by Jane Campion" appears. The camera then renders portraits of them, individually or in small groups, poised, posed, looking directly into the camera, smiling, dancing, pensive, enigmatic. The sequence ends as the camera pans down a woman's extended arm, her left palm open to us, her middle finger bearing the inscription "The Portrait of a Lady." This finger essentially points to the first shot of the narrative, a close-up of Nicole Kidman's blue eyes.

Putting Henry James's title on Campion's extradiegetic finger immediately calls to mind the opening shot of *The Piano* and its ongoing

The Portrait of a Lady title finger |

concerns with hands and fingers. It also connects Campion's imagination with James, indicating that she has read him, adapted him, for *his* fingers, for the concerns with hands and touch that run throughout his novel. Most notably, in *The Portrait of a Lady*, Isabel Archer (Nicole Kidman) establishes her singularity when she declines the economic security and social distinction inherent in the highly attractive marriage proposal of Lord Warburton (Richard E. Grant). To register both Isabel's own sense of the value of what she is refusing and the force of her ideal of independence, the narrator (in the epigraph above) uses a figure of speech to gauge what she would have given to override that refusal, that ideal—"her little finger." Narratively and thematically, Ada McGrath and Isabel Archer therefore mirror one another, albeit inversely, in their fingers and acts of refusal: if Ada gave up her literal finger rather than sacrifice her desire, Isabel would have given her figurative finger in order to feel it.[47]

The title finger and its multiple significations also apprehend the relation of a cinematic text to its literary forbear. Although Campion finds in James a kindred spirit whose novel addresses many of her own concerns, adapting the nineteenth-century literary portrait of Isabel to twentieth-century cinema requires an engagement precisely in the difference between literal and figurative fingers. The desiring body, so absent in James, so present, tactile, and visceral in Campion, marks the point wherein his figures become her fingers. Campion registers the mediation of her adaptation through the film's repeated and knowing use of historical anachronisms, the first being the contemporary antipodean women who "frame" Campion's approach to the subsequent fiction. These anachronisms formally call attention to the disparate imaginations and cultural contexts shaping the narrative and are part of the sophisticated engagement with adaptation accomplished by the film. At the same time, Campion's selection of this novel also extends her career-long investigation into the difficult truths of violence, sexuality, and the perverse conundrums of romantic love, especially for women.

In James's novel, Isabel Archer, a well-bred young woman of very modest means, travels to England from America with her aunt, Mrs. Touchett, after being orphaned when her father dies. Though Mrs. Touchett lives in Florence, she regularly visits Gardencourt, the residence of her elderly ailing husband Mr. Touchett, once a "shrewd

American banker," and her son, the sickly if acerbically charming Ralph Touchett. Both Ralph and his close friend, the wealthy, brilliant, and kind Lord Warburton, take an immediate interest in Isabel, the latter proposing marriage to her two weeks after meeting her. Isabel has already attempted to evade the attentions of an American suitor, the young inventor and industrialist, Caspar Goodwood, whose cause is being promoted by her friend, the American journalist Henrietta Stackpole. Isabel resists marriage on principle, as she is very independent and determined to have a life with the "usual chances and dangers." Inspired by her will, her cousin Ralph persuades his father to leave Isabel a fortune when he dies. Isabel's new wealth and distinction attract the attentions of Mme. Merle, an accomplished, independent woman, who recommends her young friend to Gilbert Osmond, single father to Pansy, a man of impeccable taste and no occupation. Isabel succumbs to Osmond's desire and designs, marries him, and finds herself at the novel's end the very image of all she sought to avoid.

The film begins with Isabel rejecting Lord Warburton's proposal but significantly elides the actual moment that she refuses him her *hand* in marriage. It opens with a tight close-up on Isabel's face and eyes. She could be a woman of today and only when the camera cuts to a medium shot do we travel back to a bright spring day in the late nineteenth century. In a scene that will be echoed in all its particulars at the film's close, Isabel sits within the low-lying branches of a tree and wipes away a tear (with her left, ringless hand) as the camera then cuts behind her to Warburton returning to tell her, "When I'm touched, Miss Archer, it's for life." Opening with a pronounced emphasis on hands, fingers, and being "touched," the film then follows Isabel as she rushes off across the lawn.

The next scene finds Isabel in the warm brown gloom of Mr. *Touch*ett's study, her face swimming in shadows, as she tells her uncle (John Gielgud) about Warburton's proposal and her decision to refuse it. When her uncle asks why, Isabel responds, "There was a moment when I would have given my little finger to say yes. But I think I have to begin by getting a general impression of life, and there's a light that has to dawn."[48] Isabel's dialogue, moving from hypothetical finger to anticipated light, fuses two metaphors taken directly from the novel, albeit from two different passages. The conversation is rendered in alternating close-ups rimmed in darkness that isolate Isabel's face from her body; this framing provides a neat visual counterpart to her verbal assertion about dawning light. This sequence, together with the first one, insistently contrasts darkness and light, placing this contrast in tension with a corollary emphasis on touch and tactility. The formal and psychological dynamics of the scene coalesce in Isabel's words, suggesting that this young woman, "full of theories," will be blind, and therefore susceptible, to the power and effect of fingers, of the body, of the irrational. The film materializes this problem in its simultaneous emphases on pictorial (light, shadow, image) and sensuous (fingers, movement, bodies) values.

As with *The Piano*, *Portrait* makes obsessive use of hands and fingers. Every sexual encounter in the film foregrounds hands to an inordinate degree. When Caspar Goodwood (Viggo Mortensen) comes to Isabel's rooms in London, only to be turned away by her, he runs his finger along her chin as he leaves. This gesture generates an anachronistic interpretation of Isabel's desire, a radical break with Jamesian circumspection. In the novel, the two share a "hand-clasp which was not merely passive on her side"; their confrontation leaves her "trembling—trembling all over," a reaction the narrator observes was a result of both their discussion and "simply the enjoyment she found in the exercise of her power . . . having refused two ardent suitors in a fortnight" (144–45). In the film, superimpositions render Isabel's physical reactions as an elaborate sexual fantasy in which Caspar Goodwood, Lord Warburton, and Ralph Touchett (Martin Donovan) all run their hands and fingers over her. Similarly, fingers and hands predominate in the subsequent sexual encounters between Merle (Barbara Hershey) and Osmond (John Malkovich), Isabel and Ralph, Isabel and Goodwood, as well as in all of Isabel's physical interactions (sexual, violent, or both) with Osmond. In the penultimate instance, Osmond's hand rests on his daughter Pansy's (Valentina Cervi) abdomen, his arm circling her waist, in his first "private" conversation with Isabel. This image will ominously recur, rerun in the travel/fantasy film within the film where it is Isabel's waist that Osmond grasps.

In a perceptive reading, Dale Bauer connects these hands and fingers to the large sculpture of a hand that Merle and Isabel walk by and to the small casting of a baby's hand that we see Isabel fondling deject-

Three sets of fingers on Isabel's body in
The Portrait of a Lady

edly as her maid does her hair for Osmond's Thursday soiree. Arguing that the film is as much about failed reproduction (Isabel's miscarriage, Osmond's, Merle's lost child, Campion's film) as it is repressed sexuality, Bauer underscores "Osmond's interest in copies and Isabel's in originals and her belief in self-production"; she sees all these images serving Campion's "metacommentary" on her reproduction of James's novel (195). Although extremely persuasive, this interpretation limits the reading of sexuality in this film to its issue, however failed, rather than its structure. It therefore does not account for the emphasis on seduction and sadomasochism and their association with the theme of choice throughout the film.

Campion and screenwriter Laura Jones read not only James but also scholarly work on *Portrait* to guide their adaptation. The ideas of scholars William H. Gass and Alfred Habegger so impressed Campion that she quoted them in *Portrait*'s European press kits. From William Gass, she took: "*The Portrait of a Lady* is James's first fully exposed case of human manipulation; of what it means to be a consumer of persons, and of what it means to be a person consumed" (Gordon 15). Significantly, the essay from which the quote derives opens with a meditation on touch and fiction's powerful capacity to synthesize form and the sensuous; the passage ends with the assertion that art "is charged with Being. Touching it provides a shock" (Gass 694). Gass characterizes James's central thematic concern—with humans used and made into objects—using the phrase "human manipulation," one which references a moral problem by way of the tactile or manual. "Manipulation" refers to hands, capable of touch, of skilled use, as well as "shrewd or devious management." Indeed, the word derives from *"manipulus*, or handful" (American Heritage Dictionary 794) and clearly resonates with the visual logic of such concerns imaged in *Portrait* (and, strikingly, in *The Piano* as well).

From Alfred Habeggar, Campion took a statement that she has quoted in interviews as well as the press kit: "Freedom and fatherlessness have split the heroine in two disconnected halves—a partly factitious determination to be her own master, and a dark fascination with images of dominance and submission" (Wexman, *Interviews*, 180, 187). In the essay from which this quote was taken, Habeggar bases his observation on the passage in James where Osmond and Isabel first meet in Osmond's rooms, Osmond positioning his daughter Pansy in front of him, standing between his knees, his arm around her waist.[49] Habeggar asserts that Isabel, taking in Pansy's passivity, begins to mimic it, is drawn, attracted to it: "[Isabel's] fancy has been taken by a resonant and compelling image. She is not in love yet, does not know what it feels like to desire another person. She has simply seen—been shown—a picture she cannot get out of her mind, a picture of a father and daughter" (152). It is because she does not realize how deeply abandoned she feels by her father that Isabel "is dangerously responsive to the studied self-portrait of the mutually dependent father and daughter" (159). Habeggar's reading of James proposes a similar mimetic structure to that which has informed other of Campion's films—wherein the relationship between a character who sees and one who is seen involves both imitation and sensuous connection, a relationship that transforms characters and power relationships in rationally and psychologically inscrutable ways. Such a structure brings together the pictorial and sensuous values set in tension in this film, the apt visual correlatives Campion uses to represent the conflicting forces, of theories and passions, that so beset Isabel in the film's contemporary representation of her.

That Campion used this mimetic structure to visualize Isabel's perverse choice of Osmond is evidenced in the relationship between the
two scenes that encapsulate his seduction of her, the first detailing the
act itself, the second its effect on her psyche. The first scene noticeably reverses the movement from finger to light that informed Isabel's
pronouncement to Mr. Touchett early in the film. Literally drawn into
darkness when she goes to the underground chamber in the Palazzo
Farnese to find her parasol, Isabel is startled when Osmond steps out
of the shadows with the parasol, spinning it round. The two move in and
out of the darkness and pools of light that appoint the circular chamber
as Osmond circles around Isabel. Standing off in shadow, he says, "I
find I'm in love with you." We hear a boom, the camera cuts to a long
shot away from the couple, rushing towards them, following a circular
wall appointed by a skull. Isabel responds, "No, don't say it please," but
Osmond insists, "I must say it. I'm *absolutely* in love with you," which
we hear as a loud whisper that echoes in the space around the two.
Angry and upset, she starts to leave him, and he says, "One more thing.
Would you go visit my little daughter before you leave?" Disarmed, she
smiles and reaches for her open parasol, her fingers grasping its handle
above Osmond's, but instead of releasing it, he presses one of his fingers
against hers. Each pulls, but he uses her resistance against her, drawing
her to him for a kiss, both of their hands, hers above his, clutching the
parasol. Voices cry out. Osmond runs off.

In the second scene, which registers the effects of Osmond's declaration on Isabel's psyche, Campion takes great liberties, certainly with
James, but much more notably with her own film, by using high contrast
black-and-white film stock that simulates early silent film footage to
depict Isabel's subsequent voyage with Mme. Merle to Greece, Turkey,
and Egypt. One of the two narrative sequences that drastically alters or
supplements James (the erotic fantasy scene being the other) this mock
"travel film" significantly disrupts the film's realism as well. Whereas
the erotic fantasy presents an anachronism or deviation at the level of
content—Isabel imagining herself being handled and pleasured by all
three of her suitors—the travel film within the film, titled "My Journey
1872," is multiply anachronistic, temporally at odds with or too early for
the contemporary film in which it is embedded and too late for the time
the novel represents, the 1870s (the cinema was not invented for another

two decades). Significantly, Campion calls attention to the historicity of her own medium in a sequence where she liberally embellishes James. She uses anachronism, as she has in the film's opening and the erotic fantasy scene, to highlight the different temporalities, notions of sexuality, technologies, and conventions of representation that necessarily distinguish her vision from that of James. Her film within a film does appropriately simulate the cinema in 1908, the year the revised New York edition of *Portrait* was published. Just as James, in 1908, supplemented or updated his 1881 *Portrait* with, among other things, Isabel's fear of the erotic (Mazzella 605–11), so Campion visualizes this threat and its character in this scene. In effect, she uses the cinematic history to express the novel's own evolution over nearly three decades. But this interlude also references the cinema's history in a very particular way, bringing together the two stylistic extremes that have marked it.

The scene combines straightforward "documentary" footage of Merle and Isabel on the deck of a ship, seeing pyramids in the desert, counting their luggage, and fending off begging children with "special effects" footage that uses multiple superimpositions, animation, and extreme close-ups to convey Isabel's subjective state. That is, the sequence aligns and confuses Isabel's travels (external, physical motion) and the transports of her romantic imagination (emotion), simultaneously referencing the cinema's historical fascination with the exotic and the erotic, with objective and subjective "movement." Thus, while the film within a film emulates early actualites, it also mimics the surrealists in its focus on bodies, orifices (mouths), and its evocation of the irrational and oneiric.

It begins, in long shot, with Isabel and Merle on the deck of a ship, this objective perspective quickly giving way to a subjective one, as the camera moves in closer to Isabel, who is looking at the camera, Merle standing directly behind her. We hear odd, distorted sounds as a shot of ocean waves is superimposed over that of the two women; Mme. Merle's image slowly dissolves into the water, as then does Isabel's. Their images disappear as another appears, a textured white shape around which a dark and ominous object slowly protrudes. The camera cuts back and we see it is Osmand's dark hand, huge and menacing, working its way across the white fabric of Isabel's dress, his hand slowly encircling her waist. We then see more "tourist shots" until again, the camera closes in on Isabel, on her eyes, looking out. Two reverse shots show us what she sees: first, an extreme close-up of Osmond's lips, saying "I'm absolutely in love with you," then her dish of fava beans turned into little mouths with men and women's voices, rapid, nasal, and overlapping, all saying quickly, "I'm absolutely in love with you," as flies buzz around. A statue ventriloquates Osmond's voice, then over images of the pyramids, we hear Isabel's voice, repeating as if in a stupor, a fragment of his declaration: "absolutely in love, absolutely in love."[50] Another shot depicts her suddenly looking at the camera, as we again hear his declaration. Finally, she says twice, "I'm absolutely in love with you," as we see Osmond swirling her parasol, Isabel's naked body, à la Botticelli's *The Birth of Venus*, superimposed over it, then his hand on her naked belly. Both repeat the line together as Isabel gasps, her fantasy ends, and she faints in the desert.

This scene animates Habeggar's resonant image of father and daughter within Isabel's imagination. Isabel's psyche infected with Osmond's declaration, she sees in her mind's eye not their hands on the parasol or their kiss, but rather the surreal and vaguely horrifying image of Pansy's waist become her own, with Osmond's hand creeping around it. Subsequent to this image, we begin to hear Osmond; everywhere Isabel looks, everything she looks at during her journey now is imbued with her memory, her fantasy of Osmond's mouth, his words. They echo in her mind, she repeats them, and in mimicking them, she feels a connection to him, feels his desire as it becomes her own (as she also becomes his daughter!). In this experimental sequence, Campion attempts to render cinematically the irrational conundrum of (Isabel's) desire—that it does not comply with reason, with causality, with "a light that has to dawn." But neither does it conform to the "laws of attraction." As Osmond tells Isabel, and as John Malkovich's performance makes patently clear, "he can offer her nothing." While many reviewers of the film found Osmond so obnoxious that Isabel's feelings for him were inscrutable, Campion does envision the *character* of that inscrutability—that Isabel's desire derives not from the attraction of its object (Osmond), but from her mimetic captivation by an image (of father and daughter).

In turning to the critics, Campion turns to something that is not in the novel—interpretation—to adapt its prose to a medium whose invention and consequence, she suggests, has clearly affected what we can "see" in the original text. Explicitly citing the influence of Gass and Habegger, Campion aligns her vision with late twentieth-century interpretations of the novel. The quotes she selects from each notably articulate their respective "takes" on James in reference to two different economies: that of commerce (Gass's metaphor of the "consumer and consumed"); and that of power, here sexually inflected (Habegger's notion of Isabel at once determined to be her own "master" and fascinated "with images of dominance and submission"). Economy, defined as the careful management of resources, is predicated on self-interest, a subject's control over his or her objects. If Gass used a commercial metaphor to speak to James's concern with humans used as objects, Campion uses Habegger to up the ante, making manifest the erotic economy of dominance and submission that is tacit in James, an economy in which subjects are taken as and might *choose* to be objects. She thereby explores Isabel's freedom within the narrative crosshairs of these two economies—of commerce and power—as the freedom to choose to be an object, to make a bad choice.

Ultimately Campion takes from these critics, especially Habegger, notions about James in line with her own ideas and aesthetic concerns as a filmmaker. Furthermore, in mobilizing explicit representations of sexuality, she discovers and embellishes what I would call the structure of the "perverse choice" in James. Peter Brooks identifies ethical choice as crucial to James's "melodramas of consciousness" as opposed to "melodramas of external action" that depend on suspenseful menace, pursuit, and combat. By contrast, the former generate their drama from his characters' understanding of moral problems as "pure imperatives" despite "the complications of reality" (157–59). In emphasizing Isabel's sexual desire (only alluded to in James) alongside the paradox of her self-interest and distinction as self-abnegation, Campion makes manifest the necessarily perverse character of choice for Isabel (for women) in their confronting "pure" ethical imperatives absent any consideration of the "complications of reality." Whereas in most film melodrama (by definition, "melodramas of external action"), moral certainty is derived from the spectacle of innocents tricked or deceived, Campion's *Portrait* is faithful to the perversity in James; in this film, Isabel's choices spring from "pure" imperatives whose articulation within competing economies and perspectives of "reality" render them inscrutable, perverse.

To give the most obvious example, Isabel's choice to marry Osmond is made in perfect freedom without any need for economic consideration. In novel and film, Isabel pursues her own singularity by becoming the young lady who refused "an English lord." The economic and social perversity of this choice sets her beyond both self-interest and social convention and norms. When Osmond appears with his impeccable taste, objets d'art, and submissive daughter, his distinction complements hers. Unlike her other suitors, he offers Isabel nothing, can give her nothing. In an arch appropriation of the Kantian logic of the aesthetic, Isabel experiences her choice of him as completely disinterested and therefore truly free. Paradoxically then, in the economy of marital commerce and power, the only significant and singular choice she can make is a bad or perverse one. Thus in both versions of *Portrait*, rather than the fatal coincidence that customarily animates melodrama, it is the perverse choice that shapes its heroine's fall and the narrative's brutal ironies and insights.

Campion enhances the perversity of Isabel's choice by representing what James would not and did not—her desire for Osmond, even in the context of his abuse of her. When Osmond blames her because Lord Warburton's proposal to Pansy is not forthcoming, he slaps Isabel repeatedly with his glove and trips her. Asking, "Are you satisfied?" he pushes his nose into her face and then holds his face close to hers, as if for a kiss. She turns her head tremulously to him, expectant. He pauses and then walks away. The staging suggests that Osmond withholds sex and affection to punish his wife, whereas on Isabel's side, the motivation for the clearly masochistic desire she expresses is not easily discerned. Social mores and her own allegiance to her marriage vow certainly make Osmond the only person with whom she can express or fulfill her sexual desires; now married, she has no other choice. Her desire also may or may not be related to her loss of and wish for a child—to become a mother rather than his "daughter" as she once fantasized and as Osmond now seems to desire (he has just plopped her, like a child, on a stack of cushions). In the diabolical architecture of the narrative, where Pansy, Isabel, and Merle are locked in a mise-en-abyme of mirrored identities, destinies, and desires, Isabel makes a bad choice not wholly her own, but inherited from, perversely doubled in Merle, a figure who compels Isabel's desire and prefigures her masochism.

Whereas the early scenes in *Portrait* insistently depict Isabel running, turning away, or standing aloof from the various suitors who beset her, by contrast, she moves towards Merle, literally from darkness to light when she meets her. Merle is playing the piano in a sunlit room, "just *du bout des doigts*" or "at the tip of her fingers" so as not to disturb Mr. Touchett, her presence representing a confluence of light and touch for Isabel. Subsequently, the two are inseparable, Isabel admiring, enamored, listening intently as Merle tells her that Americans "make poor Europeans," having "no natural place here," and that women have "no natural place anywhere." Merle is a role model, a mother figure, and Isabel's affection for the older woman is at least tinged with desire.

As the film continues, Merle will finally emerge as a horrifying double. The polymorphous significance of this character is emphasized by both James and Campion. She not only instigates Osmond's interest in Isabel and introduces the two, but in both, she pervades Isabel's thoughts at a signal moment. Here is James on the culmination of Isabel and Merle's voyage to the Middle East:

> Madame Merle had once declared her belief that when a friendship ceases to grow it immediately begins to decline—there being no point of equilibrium between liking more and liking less. A stationary affection, in other words, was impossible—it must move one way or the other. However that might be, the girl had in these days a thousand uses for her sense of the romantic, which was more active than it had ever been. I do not allude to the impulse it received as she gazed at the Pyramids or as she stood among the broken columns of the Acropolis; deep and memorable as these emotions had remained. She came back by the last of March and made another stay in Rome. A few days after her arrival, Gilbert Osmond descended from Florence and remained three weeks. (275)

In James, Merle and Isabel's trip takes up two pages, ending in this passage, the whole of what precedes it devoted to Isabel's reflections on Merle. Significantly, the narration moves directly from her thoughts of Merle to her active "sense of the romantic." In the novel, Isabel's "thousand uses" of the romantic are unspeakable, marked only in the text by the sources from which they do *not* derive (the Pyramids, the Acropolis). We are left to surmise their impulse by the outcome of the trip—Osmond's visit and Isabel's announcement of her engagement to him, some months later.

In Campion's visualization of the voyage, Merle stands directly behind Isabel, looking at her, as Isabel's fantasies of Osmond surface in, are superimposed on, the image of her and Merle. The film visually suggests that it is her relationship with Merle that precipitates her fantasies—Merle is literally "behind" them. Campion generates the fantastic montage of this sequence out of James's textual aporia; she puts images to Isabel's "active sense of the romantic," made up of aural and visual fragments from the film up to this point (Isabel's waist, Osmond's lips and voice) and from other films and iconic images (Botticelli's *Birth of Venus*, Hitchcock's *Vertigo*). This surreal supplement recapitulates the psychic drama of the narrative up to this point, using an oneiric logic. It functions as the hinge that joins Campion's narrative before and after Isabel's engagement to Osmond (and differs from James's, as he divides Part 1 and 2 before Osmond's declaration). Visually the dream sequence prefigures the doubling of Isabel and Merle in the latter part of the film, emphasized by the striking similarities in their hair, their clothing, their bearing, and, of course, their positions—the younger woman now replacing the other as lover and mother through the contracted position she had been determined to avoid, that of wife.

Although the film clearly portrays Isabel's passion for mastery and her captivation by the image of Osmond and the obedient Pansy, it also visualizes Merle as the precursor, the ground of this crucial transformation. In the image repertoire of the film, the first waist that Osmond lays a hand on and snakes across is not Pansy's but Merle's. In Campion's rendering, if Isabel demonstrates the desire of a masochist, her perverse choice is instigated not only by Isabel's desire for the father, but by her impulse to become, to replace, both the mother and the daughter. Early on, at the same time that Merle appears to Isabel as independence incarnate, she speaks frankly to her young friend of the difficulty of women's position; they must crawl, stay on the surface of things because they have no "natural place." Campion's Isabel draws close to, emulates the appearance of Merle, her ideal of Merle, who does all things "beautifully"; she does not attend, as James's Isabel does in part, to this crucial "key" to the older woman's "portrait of a lady" that Merle's own words offer her. Later, these same words will literally describe Isabel and her own honor-driven keeping up of appearances.

In all of Campion's films, but particularly from *The Piano* onward, mothers determine the erotic character of their daughter's relationships. In this film and her most recent, *In the Cut*, that character is profoundly masochistic, and associated with a lost or absent mother whose heartbreak and traumas are relived, repeated in their protagonist daughters' lives. *Portrait* locates Isabel's masochism in the field of what is ostensibly her choice, a field actually articulated by Merle. Osmond never really proposes to her because he does not have the resources from which to do so. Rather, he abjectly enumerates what he does not have and concludes that he offers her nothing. She, for her part, is pleased that, in addition to the disinterest of her choice, she has money enough for both of them. In terms of resources and power, she gives "everything" to Osmond's "nothing." Yet her own desire is described by James as all the things it is *not* and by Campion as an oneiric conflation of her subjectivity with that of others (Osmond, Pansy, Merle). In the blur of identification, desire, and design comprised by these characters, what Isabel cannot see is, again, the (m)other, here the other woman. She finally realizes, understands all when she asks Merle, "What have you to do with me?" and Merle tells her, "Everything."

And what does this film/story have to do with Campion? In the film's opening, the use of soft black-and-white cinematography to render the idyll in the woods cultivates a visual nostalgia that contrasts with the young women's contemporary clothing, movements, and portable Sony Walkmans. Almost without exception, these modern women articulate their relation to sexuality and sexual expression in a surprisingly passive and traditional sense; they are overpowered by it, are addicted to it, whether "it is positive, which it was at the beginning, or negative." The last voice we hear says: "It means finding a mirror, the clearest mirror, the most loyal mirror so when I love that person I know that they are going to shine that love back to me." A more apt description of Isabel's narcissistic love for Osmond could hardly be found (Murphy 29). Campion uses these voices to begin from the premise that erotic desire, especially for women, will always in some way confound choice and freedom. If, as Rebecca Gordon argues, "at the heart of James's novel there resonates a question about the very definition of the term 'independence' for a woman" (17), then Campion reframes that question, both for Isabel Archer and for her contemporary counterparts, as one that must take account of one's own sexuality and a more generalized sexual (maternal) genealogy. Though many critics have seen this opening as a sentimental paean to a "feel-good New Agey feminine community" (Polan 128), such a reading does not account for its anachronistic representation of contemporary young women, one that aligns their erotic dilemmas with those depicted in *Portrait*. Campion's highly ironic cinematic preface therefore underscores the ongoing perversity implicit in women's erotic choices and their continued sentimentalization by the contemporary young women who face her camera.

Flush from *The Piano*'s outstanding critical and financial "crossover" success, Campion herself made a perverse choice to adapt this novel. She approached *Portrait* with industry backing, the largest budget she had and would ever have to date for a film, and renowned actors, especially women, lining up to work with her.[51] Straddling what was then a fashion in both industry and feminist independent cinema—adaptations of nineteenth-century, usually British, novels[52]—she perversely chose to adapt what Rebecca Gordon aptly describes as "the notoriously unfilmable" Henry James's *The Portrait of a Lady* (14). Campion herself was aware, not only of the difficulty of adapting James's novel, but of the unpopularity of her choice, telling Rachel Abramowitz around the time of the film's release that she didn't think that many people would approve of her "following up the much-loved *The Piano* with a rendition of James's masterpiece." Reasserting her identity as an art cinema director in the face of her newfound popularity and industry funding, she told Abramowitz, "But I did this [film] for myself" (Wexman, *Interviews*, 186). Thus, with what could be seen as an Isabel Archer-ish attitude, Campion set out to make a difficult film, for herself and in accord with the imperatives of her vision, with the industry's money and imprimatur. As *Portrait* did not do well at the box office, Campion set out to make her next film, which was written with her sister Anna, for much less money. Turning to another subject difficult to render on film, she crafted *Holy Smoke* as "an essay about love, about belief systems" (quoted in Press, 1), about sexuality in relation to spirit.

Holy Smoke: **The Uses and Misuses of Touch**

In *Holy Smoke,* the third film of what could be called her "finger trilogy," Campion directs her concerns with tactility to its erotic and spiritual applications, to what it means to be "touched" in this day and age. She aligns sexuality and spirituality as pursuits people engage in to ward off what one of the film's characters refers to as the "big dark nothing." After her two historical costume dramas (and the disappointment of *Portrait*), Campion turned to contemporary comedy with *Holy Smoke,* one that updates a classical Hollywood favorite, the screwball battle of the sexes. In this comedic narrative essay on the power of different kinds of belief and truth, Campion also returns to concerns that she touched on in *Sweetie,* now giving them a global context.

The three finger films—*The Piano, The Portrait of a Lady,* and *Holy Smoke*—establish a chronological arc that situates their respective concerns with women, power, and sexuality in three complex colonial or postcolonial milieux. *The Piano* focuses on Campion's *pakeha* ancestors, Scottish colonists in mid-nineteenth-century New Zealand whose civil pretensions and romantic imaginings founder within the historical materiality of the colonial scene. *The Portrait of a Lady* uses filmic portraits and sexual testimonies of contemporary antipodean women as its ironic portal onto James's tale of a willful American naïf in Europe in the 1870s. Finally, *Holy Smoke* features just such a contemporary antipodean woman on her own journey, who forgoes the customary trip to Europe to travel to India instead. Each film opens with fingers, those we look through in *The Piano,* one that points us to the composite aesthetics of Campion's adaptation of James, and those that touch others in *Holy Smoke.*

Campion wrote the screenplay for the film with her older sister, writer and film director Anna Campion, telling interviewer Maxine McKew that Anna's agnostic stance inflected her more spiritual approach. The two sought to explore the relationship between romance and spirituality as kindred systems of belief. In their narrative, protagonist Ruth Barron (Kate Winslet) travels through India with her friend Prue (Samantha Murray) and is "touched" by guru Baba (Dhritiman Chaterji), joining his followers. Her family considers Baba a cult manipulator and they conspire to trick her into returning to Sydney, her mother traveling to Delhi with the (false) news that Ruth's father is gravely ill. Though Ruth initially refuses to leave, when her mother (Julie Hamilton) has a serious asthma attack, she escorts her home. There her family performs an intervention and, at her mother's request, Ruth agrees to go with cult deprogrammer P. J. Waters (Harvey Keitel) to an isolated hut in the outback. P. J.'s customary assistant has a family emergency and, somewhat reluctantly, he agrees to do the intervention with only Ruth's family as support. Lacking his partner, he loses his sense of autonomy, and when he and Ruth engage in pitched verbal and spiritual power struggles, their intercourse ultimately becomes sexual. Finally, Ruth attempts to run off and P. J. chases and punches her, knocking her out cold. Later, finding him devastated by his violent action, Ruth forgives him and his failure, a failure that ultimately transforms their lives and the lives of both of their families.

Holy Smoke opens with a symphony of significations, the credit sequence depicting moments from Ruth and Prue's trip to India accompanied by a concert recording (we hear the applause over a black screen) of Neil Diamond singing "Holly Holy." The song itself insinuates the hokey and the holy and sets the stage for two very distinct but related tactile encounters. As Diamond croons, the visuals depict the inside of a crowded bus, many people standing, and two hands, one black, one white, pressed on the roof. The camera moves back, showing us Ruth, as an Indian man reaches out from behind her and caresses her neck. She brushes his hand away, and we cut to smoke from cooking wafting up to the title, "Holy Smoke." An extended montage follows in which a group of sari-clad Western women, embracing one another, laughing and talking as they walk along, catch Ruth's eye as she drinks coffee with Prue. The sequence culminates in Ruth arguing with Prue about pursuing the guru whose followers these women are. Prue is frightened but Ruth is intrigued. Ruth tells Prue, "I really want to do this. It's some of the real stuff."

On the next cut, the film moves to San Souci, Sydney, where we see Prue hurrying to the house of Ruth's parents. Once in their living room, she begins to tell them what transpired in India. As the image track shifts back to Delhi, Prue's voiceover recounts the story of Ruth's enlightenment in her encounter with Baba. While Prue narrates the event as a terrible crisis—"but it was scary . . . some kind of freaky hypnotism happened"—the images we see render a more ambiguous version. Ruth and Prue sit in a crowd of chanting, swaying disciples, the focus blurred save for the center of the screen, where we see Prue, off to the side looking terrified, and Ruth, centered, happy, and engaged. Baba makes his way through the crowd toward Ruth, reaching out to her. As he touches her forehead, she falls back, swooning in ecstasy. Her third eye opens and tears roll down her face, the image depicting an explosion of brightly colored lotus flowers, clouds, eyes, and butterflies (which we later see on the wall of Ruth's bedroom) radiating around Ruth's head.

Thus *Holy Smoke* begins with two touches: one furtive, trivial, sexual, and transgressive, an anonymous caress; the other fated (Baba picks her out among the crowd), profound, sacred, and transformative. Baba's touch not only transforms Ruth but also the film's mise-en-scène, which moves from the realistic to the fantastic to register his effects on her in the visual rhetoric of Bollywood, the world's largest film industry, located in Bombay.[53] Both encounters take place between an Indian man and a white Australian woman in a very specific postcolonial milieu: Australia and India were both colonies of Britain. Yet as the opening of *Holy Smoke* makes clear in its staging of these two instances of physical

Baba's touch on Ruth's forehead in *Holy Smoke* |

contact between differently gendered and raced subjects of empire, the status of these three participants is neither equal nor stable. For Ruth, the racialized sexual touch is annoying, unwanted, and transgressive, but it can also be brushed off; the racialized spiritual touch is desired and exoticized, a profound escape from the stifling and claustrophobic normalcy of her life in Sans Souci.

Yet lest we, like Ruth, idealize her orientalist spiritual escape, Campion sets this opening to the catchy swells of the Neil Diamond pop song that exemplifies in its title ("Holly Holy") the blurring of sexuality and spirituality the film addresses. Its compelling banality accomplishes two interrelated effects: it imbues the sequence with delirious wit and affect while it also testifies to a certain kind of projective pop orientalism that locates spirituality in "the East," a projection Campion makes manifest and deconstructs by having the Diamond song "become" diegetic, the accompaniment for ecstatic dancing among Baba's mostly white, mostly Western faithful on a rooftop in Delhi.

The film also tacitly links Diamond and Baba and their respective culture industries, the latter which facilitate pop star and guru's "move" across the globe, as well as their ability to "move" and to "touch" people who are their fans or disciples. The applause that opens the film signals that the recording of Diamond is "live." Similarly, Prue remarks to Ruth's parents that she and Ruth had merely "wanted to visit a real live guru." Though the mass adulation for guru and pop star depends upon an equivalence between the live and the real or true, the film cannily registers that the force of this equivalence paradoxically depends precisely on film and music industries that manage representation and recording as well as the cultural stereotypes they foster (in seeking "a real live guru," Ruth and Prue sought a copy of what they already knew). Thus *Holy Smoke* both documents and engages in the performance and exchange of pop culture as commodity and stereotype that is nevertheless capable of provoking ecstatic (secular or religious) experience. Combining the comic and the cosmic, the supernatural with the supranational, the film traces different modes of touching and being touched, considering how they animate relations among individuals as well as motivate cultural and ideological exchange among nations.

Campion triangulates the postcolonial encounter her film initially stages between Australia and India with America, insistently registering the latter's influence in the U.S. pop songs that dominate the soundtrack and in the characters of P. J. Waters and his assistant Carol, played by Harvey Keitel and Pam Grier, who fly in to "rescue" Ruth from Indian enlightenment.[54] Imported from Hollywood, Keitel and Grier are at once associated with mainstream genre films (action) as well as with different variants of U.S. independent or "cult" cinemas: he with the alternative productions of New Hollywood and she with blaxploitation. Ruth's "Bollywood" revelation at Baba's hands therefore instigates complex gender, generational, racial, and cultural conflicts that complicate and destabilize any easy or facile understanding of the power dynamics Campion depicts among various characters. In effect, P. J. Waters displaces Baba, who has in turn replaced Ruth's father (Tim Robertson) and his authority in relation to her. Thus, in *Holy Smoke*, the investigation of sexual, spiritual, and pop cultural touching takes place in the context of certain transference relationships that Campion stages with older male characters in the power position (as father, spiritual leader, therapist and deprogrammer) and a younger female character as subject to that position (as daughter, disciple, and client). In these transference relationships, physical and sexual touch are proscribed while this power, through sublimation, fuels the transformations such relationships produce.

Campion links these relations by various means—"Baba" means "father"; Ruth comes back from India because of her mother's breakdown and her father's supposedly imminent demise; P. J. Waters begins his work with Ruth by engaging and trying to master her in discussions of philosophy and spirituality. In all these relationships, gender and power positions are explicitly marked in a millennial battle of the sexes that Campion also construes as a battle between generations. Campion again takes up a genre or narrative mode associated with women and gender—here a comic battle of the sexes or, as Polan terms it, screwball comedy (149)—and transforms it in the film's narration. For example, at the level of the narrative, having a large age disparity between P. J. and Ruth allows Campion to invert certain gender stereotypes. Rather than having Ruth be vain and vulnerable about her looks, these concerns about appearance and worth plague P. J. (a feature that helps explain why so many male critics dismissed the film, outraged at how "unfair" the match between the two was).

In a certain sense, *Holy Smoke* takes up where *The Piano* left off.

The earlier film's concerns with patriarchy, misogyny, colonialism, and their connection to repression and sexuality are moved forward in time. In *The Piano*, Campion investigates female sexuality as a powerful, frightening, and willful force. In so doing, she exerted her imagination against a claustrophobic colonial Victorian past and invented a new unromanticized genealogy for herself (as a *pakeha* New Zealander). In *Holy Smoke*, she investigates contemporary female sexuality in relation to spirituality as an avenue to power and escape. As anthropologist Piya Chatterjee observes, "It is no accident that Campion mines a tradition [Indian] that from the beginning has seen spirituality and sexuality as completely entwined and has revered and, more importantly, feared the power of the female principle and female sexuality."[55]

Campion blends her borrowings from Hinduism with biblical references as well. Though *Holy Smoke* appears to map a male/female gender binary on one opposing Eastern spirituality and Western materialism and sexuality, Ruth's biblical antecedent, among other things, suggests a more complex reading. The biblical Ruth forgoes her own god and native land to profess loyalty to her mother-in-law Naomi after both lose their husbands. Vowing to Naomi that "whither thou goest, I will go," Ruth travels with her, and by dint of the younger woman's physical labor and sexual sacrifice, both seen as marks of her spiritual worth, regains for Naomi her deceased husband's patrimony (Ruth 1:14–4:17). Significantly, the biblical Ruth's story blends sexuality and spiritual worth and emphasizes the value of relationships and loyalty between women. Set against the gendered struggles and couples that seem to dominate this film are many relationships, ranging from the affectionate to the erotic, among women. Like her antecedent, Ruth helps her mother regain her occupation (as veterinarian) and her dignity when her marriage to Ruth's philandering father breaks up. She and her mother remain a family, traveling back to India together, the two living and working together with Ruth's new boyfriend on animal rescue.

Within the narrative arc of *Holy Smoke*, Campion traces the pitched battle of gender and generation across the three sections into which the film is divided, each distinguished by different modes of narration, deception, and conflict. The first section, described above, takes place primarily in Delhi and concerns stories and their reliability. The cult expert who initially outlines the problem and strategy of deprogramming to Ruth's parents aptly captures the fundamental power struggle latent in any sense of belief or truth. He explains, "They [gurus, seers, cult leaders] make up their little stories, we make up ours." Campion highlights what is at stake in this contest between "their" stories and "ours" in several ways. She casts doubt on Prue's initial narration and the story she tells in the obvious contrast between what Prue says and what we see on screen. She hilariously underscores the gross disparity between Ruth's story of enlightenment and her family's story of their "golden girl" when her mother Miriam gives her the false news that her father is dying. Ruth weeps, rapturously observing how she could never cry before, and then tells her mother, "Well, maybe next time"—that is, that she will have to see her father again in some future life. Finally, Campion ironizes the very story she is telling in this first section by recounting Miriam's "passage to India" replete with a hysterical breakdown—an obvious allusion to earlier stories of colonial encounters. Locating deception, self- and otherwise, in *all* the characters and their stories within this initial section, Campion troubles any stable understanding of or conventional distinction between "us" and "them," but never allows difference in its myriad forms to disappear from the screen.

Back in Sydney, the film's second section begins with Ruth's return home and the arrival of P. J. Waters, an arrival accompanied by another Neil Diamond song, "I Am, I Say," an anthem to rugged individualism if ever there was one. In contrast to the first section and its emphasis on competing stories, the second one introduces the theme of the agenda, specifically P. J.'s three-day deprogramming schedule (we hear his voiceover: "Sydney, Australia: Case number 190") that he lays out for Ruth's family: "Day One—isolate the subject, get her attention and her respect." The text of P. J.'s agenda then becomes the content of his voiceover, dividing up by day and by programmatic step the visual narration of his struggle with Ruth at the Half Way Hut. But the programmatic agenda of P. J.'s master narrative goes badly awry, his agenda derailed, ironically, by its very success. P. J.'s narration moves from the assurance of "The cracks widen, the client falls apart. Bye, bye, Baba," to "Day Three—Oh shit!" as Campion throws into stark relief the difference between the apparent and the operant power relations in the clash between the two. Whereas P. J.—older, professional, male—has the added advantages of control over Ruth's environment ("isolate her") and her family's and, especially devastating for Ruth, her mother's sanction, Ruth comes to the contest of wills with brains, wit, beauty, and youth, together with a "ruthlessness" that P. J. cannot match.

As with Ada's extrarational will in *The Piano*, the battle that transpires between Ruth and P. J. is less a matter of their calculation than of their "acting out"—in seductions, transgressions, and violations whose consequences dramatically shift the balance of power back and forth between them. Ruth, emboldened with her own intelligence, youth, beauty, and sexuality, attacks P. J.'s masculinity, ridiculing his middle-aged vanities: "There's no way I can listen to anyone like you who dyes their hair." The crisis that then ensues between "the client falls apart," and "oh shit!" does indeed involve Ruth breaking down. She loses her belief, her center, and in her very agitated state, she attempts to seduce P. J., who initially resists but then succumbs to her utter vulnerability. His violation of that vulnerability and transgression of his professional responsibility result in her loss of respect for and sexual dominance over him. At his request, "Ok, I'm going to lie down and I want you to do your worst," she humiliates him, dressing him up in drag (she makes him into "just the girl" for him), and then jumps up and down, saying "I've won, I'm on top, I'm the winner." He concedes the battle, but just as quickly, the tables again turn. Telling her that her "physical superiority makes her cruel," he says he will tell her who she is. He writes backwards on her forehead, "Be kind," a message she must look in the mirror to read. Ruth, devastated, sees her own defeat in this inscription—the Dalai Lama's message appearing on her forehead as P. J.'s indictment of her cruelty. But Campion does not stop there. P. J. shamelessly exploits his own triumph and Ruth's confession that she fears she is heartless by saying, "I hope that you're heartless enough to abuse me for your own sick pleasure." After the two have sex again, Ruth, disgusted and overwhelmed, attempts to run off with shoes she has fashioned from ribbon and books (P. J. has confiscated her footwear to prevent her from escaping).

From the beginning of the film, the supposed investments of various characters in overarching ideals, morality, or altruism are revealed as thin pretexts for their fundamentally self-interested drives for control and power. Ruth's family wants her deprogrammed because her interest in Baba threatens them and the spiritual paucity of their lifestyle; it

P. J.'s inscription, "Be Kind," in *Holy Smoke* |

inspires in them a racialized sexual paranoia repeatedly referenced in the film. They hire P. J. to un-touch her, to restore her to a vapid and soulless normalcy. But P. J.'s influence is neither selfless nor disinterested either. His narcissistic investment in his own mastery and masculinity compels him to take the bait in Ruth's sexual mockery. Campion also undercuts Ruth's perspective as she moves from an exoticized and racialized paternal transference (Baba) to a combative, secularized one (P. J.), clearly depicting Ruth's own faith, her conversion, as deeply self-interested. Ruth embraces the touch of the other as a defense against her own life and its claustrophobic dimensions and future. Her swoon, her thrall to Baba elicits a chain of compensatory actions wherein each participant—Ruth's family, P. J., Ruth herself—lays claim to higher morals or truths than the others against whom they struggle. The film sets up these positions of *ressentiment* only carefully to expose the profoundly vested self-interest of everyone involved.

The vertiginous shifts of power that characterize P. J. and Ruth's relationship ultimately present an obverse instance where an altogether different kind of "physical superiority" results in cruelty. P. J. chases after Ruth, hanging on to her to stop her from leaving him. She slaps him off, yet unlike the Indian man on the bus who accepted Ruth's brush-off, P. J. does not. In retaliation for her rejection, he punches her with such force that he knocks her out. As in *The Piano* where Stewart attacks Ada with an ax, a sequence whose graphic visuals and sound make it one of the more viscerally violent in the cinema, Campion uses sound and slow motion to underscore the force of this punch. Like Stewart's mutilation of Ada, P. J.'s act of physical violence is inexcusable. Yet while Campion emphasizes the trauma of each of these moments, she resolutely refuses to use either act as the basis for a moral or truth that would resolve the narrative. Rather, she traces how these acts skew or pervert the power relations out of which they come.

In this, one of Campion's strategies for avoiding gendered *ressentiment* might be seen as an example of what Gayatri Spivak calls an enabling violation—a violation whose terms and consequences provide the basis—albeit contaminated—for subsequent resistance against a perpetrator. Identifying the "enabling violations" of British imperialism, Spivak stresses that the violation is never undone or attenuated but its effects enable positions of identification or power from which resistance can be mobilized. For Spivak, nothing is prior to or outside the scene of violation for the violated whose subjectivity within the imperial relation is cast within that scene. In her development of this concept, she notes how Western intellectuals lack knowledge of the history of imperialism and defines this lack, what is not known about their own history and complicity, as "the epistemic violence that constituted/effaced a subject that was obliged to cathect (occupy in response to desire) the space of the Imperialists' self-consolidating other" (209). Stewart's marriage to, incarceration of, and mutilation of Ada, not to mention Baines's bargains and blackmail with her piano, especially function in this way as their violations precipitate her desire, her will to live, her reacquisition of speech, and her ultimate assumption of a normalized identity. Most significant about Campion's narration is that the effects of these violations are registered without the narrative signaling any moral or epistemic compensation or resolve.

In the case of *Holy Smoke*, Campion's positioning of Ruth differs significantly from her conception of Ada as ancestor, trapped in interlocked matrices of oppression and repression. What threatens Ruth, a genealogical descendent of Ada's, is precisely the normalcy that Ada attains. Ruth enters the struggle with P. J. with a power differential that still exists but that is comparatively attenuated in relation to that experienced by Ada. Campion explicitly foregrounds Ruth's youth and sexuality as significant components of her power over P. J. and also emphasizes Ruth's awareness of and readiness to use this power. Yet the beginning and ending of *Holy Smoke*'s second section are marked by two moments of formal narration that clarify the exact nature of Campion's intervention in the schema of violence and difference she puts forth in this film.

The formal narration framing the introduction of P. J., a white American male—Neil Diamond's "I Am, I Say"—signals via pop rhetoric the fantasy of a Cartesian subject whose being is coextensive with its assertion. This autonomous, self-assured notion, ironized both by the visual introduction of P. J. and the ensuing narrative, is answered by the altogether different model of knowing manifested in the inscription P. J. places on Ruth's forehead. Only through the agency and gaze of the other can Ruth look in a mirror and truly see herself. P. J.'s imperative, that Ruth "be kind" calls upon her to cease being "ruth-less" and to become herself, become kind, by looking in the mirror. (The archaic meaning of the word *ruth* is compassion or pity). This scene allegorizes the psychoanalytic and therapeutic understanding of the self, wherein insight and self-knowledge can only be attained in collaboration with another. Politicizing this allegory, Campion replaces the therapeutic other of the analyst with an adversarial other marked by difference in gender, age, nationality, and power position. Thus, although these two moments of formal narration (like Ruth, we can read what P. J. has written only when she looks in the mirror) articulate very different conceptions of knowledge and self-possession, only the second incorporates difference as crucial in understandings of the self and truth.

Yet Ruth's moment of revelation does not lead to redemption; rather, her self-recognition fills her with revulsion and vertigo. When she flees, P. J. stops her by knocking her out. His act of violence ultimately leads to his total breakdown when Ruth does escape him and he collapses in the outback. In a scene which mirrors Ruth's "Indian vision" at the beginning of the narrative, P. J. hallucinates her as a Hindu goddess strolling lurid and majestic on the horizon, a vision accompanied by "Baby, It's You" on the soundtrack. His delusion, deifying the object of his desire, mirrors her spiritualizing the touch of the other.[56] While the Indian deity is clearly depicted as P. J.'s delusional point of view within the narrative, the pop song enunciates Campion's narrational voice, a voice that wittily but decisively opens up the diegesis, as have other musical selections throughout the film. Rather than soliciting our full emotional immersion in the moment depicted, as film music customarily does, Campion uses this song both for its allure and for the disjunction it creates with the visual track to generate extra-diegetic affect. This strategy distances the spectator from the narrative, but not in the mode of Brecht or Godard. Rather the distance derives from a comic sense of incongruity laced with the pleasure and nostalgia elicited by the song. Working in tandem with the music, the cinematography borrows saturated color and Hindu iconography from Bollywood to add yet another layer of signification to this ludic commentary.

This second section culminates in a scene where P. J. writhes in pain and delirium in the back of a pickup truck as Ruth sits in front with her two brothers and her sister-in-law. Ruth looks back at P. J., bruised, dirty, ridiculous in the tattered remains of the red dress, and she demands that her brother stop the truck. She gets in the back with P. J., holding him, being kind of her own volition.

P. J. hallucinates Ruth as Kali in *Holy Smoke*

In the third and brief final section of *Holy Smoke*, the narrational mode becomes one of *correspondence*, relayed by Ruth and P. J.'s sequential voiceovers, each narrating the contents of postcards they mail to the other. Ruth is in Jaipur, India, and P. J. in Seattle, U.S.A. We see the image from a postcard and its text swimming on screen in a series of dissolves that finally resolves into an image of Ruth. Initiating the exchange, she brings P. J. up to date on her life a year after their encounter with one another. Her father ran off with his secretary, and Ruth now lives in Jaipur doing animal rescue work with her new boyfriend and her mother. She is still chasing the truth, and has read the complete Bhagavad Gita. She ends by saying, "I don't know why I love you, but I do, from afar. Something really did happen, didn't it? Ruth."

Again in a series of dissolves rendering the text of his letter, P. J. answers her, as the image resolves into Ruth's postcard, bearing the image of a Hindu goddess, propped against his computer screen. He writes of having twins with his wife, Carol, and of their reconciliation after his affair with Ruth. Ruefully, he tells her he is writing a novel about a man who meets his avenging angel. He then finishes by saying: "About the something, didn't you notice it just about killed me? Yours anytime (don't tell Carol), P. J."

Several things are striking about these final sequences. First, dominated by text and voiceover, the image track in them faithfully illustrates rather than contests what we are hearing. With images and the voices in dialogue, each character concedes the influence and power of the other while each narrates a differently experienced (lack of) resolution. For Ruth, their encounter, like her encounter with Baba, is a mystery, a "something," an event that was profound, yet somewhat inscrutable. This "something" is a larger story than the conflict between "little stories" with which the film opened. For P. J., his near-death experience was life-altering—he has become (pro)creative and is no longer completely trapped in adolescent masculine agendas, scores, and vanities.

Finally, then, there is *no* answer. "Something" happened, the verification of which Ruth seeks from P. J. Yet that something, a violent, traumatic exchange, an event rather than a determinative outcome, cannot be articulated or named. In the film's rendering, Ruth's moment of self-recognition, the violence and the transformations that ensue occur not as testament to some larger truth or moral that could be believed or held onto, but as accidental or contingent consequences of vested conflicts based on self-interest and desire. The film, like Ruth, has traveled from Sans Souci ("without mercy") to a search without an end, to a resolution, spurred by kindness, and made up only of an exchange of correspondences.

Holy Smoke's meditation on spiritual and sexual touching, on the aspirations of the body to these different types of transcendence and the fine line between them, occurs within a narrative that humorously references many supranational media that have repeatedly mined this fine line: Bollywood cinema, American pop music and cinema, avant-garde and independent filmmaking. Answering back to its own opening, the film ends with P. J.'s voice and a biracial domestic scene—P. J. narrates his new life as husband to Carol and father of twins as we see Carol with him in their bedroom, both attending to their babies. While the biracial, transnational touching at the beginning of the film occurred in the context of spiritual/sexual tourism, here that touch becomes domestic in a sense that exceeds the scene depicted. The film ends with the two characters and actors imported from the fringes of Hollywood, significantly in the role of cult deprogrammers. As actors, both Grier and Keitel have careers whose early success in cult and independent films waned, but then experienced a significant resurgence in the 1990s. Their creative renaissance and coupling ends the film with a note of optimism regarding the combinations possible in global and domestic film industries indicative of this cultural moment.

These cross-cultural allusions structure a film whose voiceover narration shifts from female character to male character, finally culminating in an epistolary exchange in voiceover that ends the film. Campion systematically undercuts the reliability of her voiceover narrators and her protagonist until the correspondence at the end. She does so by contrasting the visual rendering of various events with the versions of them asserted by her voiceover narrators: first Prue, then P. J., neither of whose narration can contain or fully apprehend the narrative we see taking place. The voiceovers that then resolve the narrative—the content of two postcards sent by Ruth and P. J. to each other—transform struggles for mastery into an exchange of concessions.

Campion has consistently employed female narration to retell stories conventionally associated with women or women's issues. Yet in each instance, she marks what exceeds the knowledge and perspective of these narrators. For example, in *Sweetie*, Gordon's perspective cannot be apprehended or articulated by Kay, and in *The Piano*, Ada's final words are not hers, but those of Thomas Hood, whose poem (selected for the film by Campion's mother, Edith) she recites (a poem significantly about silence). In *Holy Smoke*, Ruth and P. J.'s final exchange affirms the transformational power of a bad choice, a bad match, a doomed love affair utterly dependent on the contingencies of the moment. In taking on our related drives for passion and for meaning and their systematic confusion, *Holy Smoke* stresses the transitory and ephemeral quality of the goals of these drives. Rather than belief in "the one," be that one a deity or a romantic partner, the film holds out only the value of the search and the incommensurate correspondences that take place along the way.

In the Cut: **Adaptation, Grief, and Closure**

> It's a film with grief around it—people with hearts who aren't satisfied, but they're searching.
>
> —Jane Campion

Jane Campion's most recent film, *In the Cut* (2003), disarticulates what she refers to as "the romantic myth in western society" by mobilizing it within the context of a self-reflexive noir thriller (quoted in Fuller 16). The film is a summing up, a resolving, and represents both a deviation from and a culmination of visual and thematic concerns that have spanned Campion's filmmaking career. Gone is the explicit emphasis on fingers and on women whose lives are transformed by travel, whether to the outback, Europe, the colonies, the Middle East, or India. *In the Cut* begins and stays in and around post-9/11 New York City, its thirty-something heroine confined to local transit and the transports of her imagination. Though Campion has repeatedly staged and transformed industry genre conventions (melodrama, gothic) in the context of art cinema, *In the Cut* is her first clear-cut genre film, one much more graphically sexual and violent than any of her other films.[57] At the same time, in the film's source text, Susanna Moore's 1995 novel of the same title, Campion found an imagination that could be the double of her own. Moore's "literary erotic thriller" features an aesthetically sophisticated first-person female narrator. A writer, reader, and investigator of language, she becomes caught up in complicit mysteries of sexuality and violence. The object of several men's attention, she ultimately chooses between two tall, dark, and handsome men, perfect doubles—the one a lover, the other a killer. She makes a bad choice.

The narrator, Frannie Avery (Meg Ryan), is a teacher obsessed with both poetry and slang; words rather than people "thrill" her. Save for her close friend Pauline (Jennifer Jason Leigh), friend John (Kevin Bacon), and Afro-Caribbean student Cornelius (Sharrieff Pugh), who serves as a slang informant for her research, Frannie is a loner. She is simultaneously drawn into an affair and a murder investigation when, meeting Cornelius in a bar to discuss his course writing assignment, she opens the wrong door on the way to the bathroom and sees a woman giving a man a blow job. Though she never sees the man's face clearly, she does note a three of spades tattoo on his wrist. The woman later turns up dead, "disarticulated" by a serial killer, and a Detective Malloy (Mark Ruffalo) shows up at Frannie's apartment. With a New Yorker's (and the genre's) reflexive suspicion, Frannie denies she knows or saw anything, but nevertheless, inscrutably, starts seeing Malloy, who has a three of spades tattoo on his wrist. She meets his partner and buddy, Rodriguez (Nick Damici), who looks just like him, but whose misogyny brings out the worst in Malloy. One night, Frannie is mugged by a masked man who she thinks is the killer. A passing cab saves her life, and Malloy comes to her rescue; they sleep together, have great sex, but when she tells him about seeing him at the bar, receiving sexual services, he denies it.

Frannie, drawn to but mistrusting Malloy, goes to stay with her friend Pauline, as the mugger has her address (he stole her purse). Then Pauline is murdered. Grief-stricken and drunk, Frannie kisses Cornelius when he stops by to express his sympathy about her friend's death, but then she rejects him, enraging him. She then has sex with Malloy after handcuffing him. Going to his jacket pocket for the key to release him, she finds the bracelet charm she had lost when she was mugged. Despite Malloy's assertions to the contrary, the charm confirms her lurking suspicions that he is the killer. She runs out of her apartment and into the arms and car of Rodriguez, who takes her to a lighthouse under the George Washington Bridge. When they arrive, she sees that he also has a three of spades tattoo and understands that he is the killer. In the novel's horrific ending, Frannie narrates her own death at Rodriguez's hands, signaled in the shift from first- to third-person in the last line of the text. In the film, she has Malloy's jacket with her and she kills Rodriguez with Malloy's gun. The film ends as she rejoins Malloy in her apartment and the door shuts on the camera.

The fundamentals of Moore's story (a woman caught between two men who are "doubles"; bad choices made in relation to sex and violence), its structure (first-person female narration), and its use of literary allusions to reflect on and inflect the genre it employs all echo salient concerns in Campion's oeuvre. Campion's filmmaking consistently foregrounds female interiority through permutations of female narration, especially in the use of voiceover, and in stories about erotic attraction, antagonism, and violence. Her first three feature films each have singular female narrators: *Sweetie* uses Kay's voiceover and perspective to indicate how that perspective has been shaped by what exceeds her knowledge; *Angel* features Janet Frame making herself a "first person" against unspeakable odds; and *The Piano* chronicles narrator Ada's jettisoning of a self-enclosed colonial imaginary and her ascension to spoken language. In Campion's next two features, male and female voiceovers interact. In *Portrait,* Isabel's mind echoes with Osmond's declaration to her, her inner speech finally mimicking him, infecting her with his desire, and in *Holy Smoke*, the pitched conflict between stories, between male and female narrational voices becomes a dialogue, a correspondence at film's end. Thus, Campion's work systematically explores the environmental, interpersonal, and self-inflicted constraints to self-knowledge, expression, and eroticism that confront her protagonists as they attempt to assume and interact in the "first person."

In this sense, Campion's selection to adapt a novel in which a woman narrates her own violent death through a declension from first person to third constitutes an endpoint in her sustained exploration of female narration under duress. Like James's "notoriously unfilmable" *The Portrait of a Lady*, which Moore's novel references, her ending, which Campion said "shattered" her, was undoable, unfilmable, albeit for different reasons than for *Portrait*. In an acknowledgement of Hollywood genre and star conventions, Campion noted that no studio would fund it: "Frannie lives or the movie dies. So you had to find a way for her to survive and still keep it bare" (Quinn 1–2). To do so, Campion collaborated with Moore on the script and they changed the ending. Other significant changes were made as well, their collaboration greatly expanding the theme of the double, Pauline's role, and Frannie's backstory, all intertwined in the family romance added to the film. Pauline becomes Frannie's beloved and abject half-sister, her double, their familial and psychic bond to each other forged in the traumas suffered by their mothers at the hand of their father. Whereas he impulsively proposed to, married, and suddenly deserted Frannie's mother, killing her with grief as he moved on to another of his four wives, he didn't even marry Pauline's mother. Their mothers' experiences have left them differently damaged; while Pauline sleeps with and stalks married men, wanting to marry just once "for her mother," Frannie is shut down, repressed; her desires incline to words, to imagination, not to romance or marriage. The two daughters therefore become doubles for their mothers as well as for each other. The family romance plot significantly recasts the focus of this noir thriller from *single urban woman in peril* to *mothers and daughters at risk,* and thus the "freedom to make poor choices" endemic to the crime narrative (Kirn 9) is here set in the context of romance, family genealogy, trauma, and repetition.

This subplot also locates the film in the industry tradition of noir/ family melodrama hybrids such as *Mildred Pierce, Strangers on a Train,* and *It's a Wonderful Life;* it differs from these films insofar as *In the Cut* emphasizes the equivalence between these two generic worlds in relation to women's position within them. It not only domesticates and familializes the parallel constructed in Moore's text between eroticism and murder, but it also infuses *In the Cut* with Campion's longstanding creative interests in sisters, daughters, and mothers—interests, it turns out, shared by Moore. *In the Cut* was the first novel Moore wrote that did *not* focus on female family members. Her previous novels, her Hawaiian trilogy, featured mothers, sisters, and daughters who desert, fail, and betray one another, whose love for one another is, as in Campion's films, frequently tragically misguided. Campion's and Moore's imaginative interests are uncannily similar in other ways as well. Both artists contend with the colonial histories of their homelands, New Zealand and Hawaii, but do so within the confines of erotic and familial relations. Each artist also admires Henry James and creatively engages with his Isabel Archer.

Moore has Frannie live on what she thinks of as "the Henry James side" of Washington Square (even though she knows he never actually lived on the square) (Moore 10),[58] and her character shares at least one telling biographical detail with James's Isabel: both were left by their widowed fathers in a European hotel when each was in their early teens (Isabel eleven, Frannie thirteen). Frannie and Isabel make bad choices in men, and Moore emulates James in a marked penchant for irony, the mode in which each author registers the force of their respective heroines' questionable decisions.

Moore's highly self-reflexive erotic thriller opens with Frannie musing on her students' difficulties understanding irony. She considers assigning them various "ironic" tutor texts (Naipaul's *Bend in the River* or *Guerillas;* Greene's *Brighton Rock*), but decides against it because she speculates that, in reacting to the violence against women in them, the students might miss their irony and intelligence. She remembers in *Brighton Rock*, "the dream in which the murderer, straight razor in hand, says: 'Such tits'" (3). Frannie's reflections at the outset of the novel presciently script her own death at its end, and lay a reflexive ironic snare for its readers. As Frannie discovers, getting lost in the cut between apparent and intended meaning can have fatal consequences. Her death can therefore be read either as a critique of her initial reflections, insofar as the nuances of irony cannot save her from the reality of brute violence, or as a critique of negative reader responses. Readers offended by *In the Cut*'s violence against women, this opening implies, are like Frannie's students, sensible, but unsophisticated, incapable of appreciating the novel's irony and intelligence.

Campion's film redirects the novel's honed reflexivity to issues concerning adaptation and genre, both "double-voiced" structures that involve reduplication, repetition, and genealogy. As with her other features, the film's opening credit sequence provides a rich visual and thematic overture as key to the film that follows, highlighting in this instance doubles, ambivalence, repetition, trauma, mothers and daughters, and the present haunted by the past. In a series of brief shots, we see dystopic, downscale, Lower East Side Manhattan in the early morning, each image, like those in the opening of *An Angel at My Table*, fading to black. The first shot, initially blurred, comes into focus, depicting the lower Manhattan skyline haunted by the absence of the twin towers.

(The film was shot in Manhattan the summer after 9/11). We then see: a building-size billboard of a woman's face, her profile doubled, looking both ways; graffiti of a face, with pinwheel eyes and a jagged mouth, seen through bars; a pile of garbage next to a fence; and a line of garbage cans next to a red flower painted on a dirty sidewalk.

Throughout, the theme of mothers and daughters is registered aurally by a "downscale" rendition of "Que Será, Será" accompanied by a very distinct, discordant piano score.[59] As the daughter/singer's questions shift from her mother ("What will I be?") to her teacher ("What should I try?"), the fades cease and the film begins to move in a shot that echoes the opening shot of *Sweetie*. From a high angle, the camera captures a woman's high-heeled shoes and lacy hemmed black dress as she negotiates an uneven sidewalk. Were it night, the deserted streets, the camera angle, the heels would, by the law of the genre, mean the woman's certain death. Like Moore's novel, then, Campion's film begins by presciently marking the woman who will die, but unlike her, she opens with Pauline, a supporting character, not Frannie, the protagonist, the camera moving up and around to an extreme close-up of her, an echo of the close-ups that introduce young Janet Frame in *Angel* and Isabel Archer in *Portrait*. The camera cuts back as Pauline steps into an urban garden, sips her coffee, fascinated and distracted, like Ruth in the opening sequence of *Holy Smoke*, here by a man practicing tai chi. She then turns her face up to a sudden shower of flowers raining down on her as the title song, which recurs in various forms throughout the film, shifts to a lush instrumental flourish. We cut then to the petal shower from inside a window, in front of which butterflies (like those in *Holy Smoke*) float in a mobile.

This first part of the credit sequence contains shots whose subject and framing recall the opening moments of each of Campion's feature films, save *The Piano*, which is eerily invoked throughout by the dissonant piano that accompanies the theme song. These allusions associate Pauline with Campion's previous protagonists and their memory (*Angel*), inner voice (*Sweetie, The Piano*), choice (*Portrait*), or spiritual curiosity (*Holy Smoke*), but unlike them, Pauline is older, world weary—reviewers repeatedly referred to her as "bruised." The camera then cuts to Frannie, sleeping, rolling over to face the petal shower outside her window. Her eyes open, close, and then the image blurs, as we see, in

Shoes in *Sweetie* |

A visual quotation—shoes in *In the Cut* |

the cut between waking and dream, "Directed by Jane Campion." In the dream, shot in sepia-toned black-and-white, the white of the pillow becomes ice on which a young woman pirouettes on ice skates; the frame becomes a man's arm, hand in leather glove, his fist clenching. He skates off toward the young woman, circles around her, then sweeps into the foreground of the shot, the cut of his skate bleeding red underneath the film's title. (We will later learn that Frannie's dream depicts the scene of her parents' betrothal.) Altogether this sequence blends multiple references to doubles with the passive, fatalistic lyrics of "Que Será, Será" and gorgeously rendered images of ambivalence—flowers and garbage, heat and cold, waking and dream—renditions that end in ice and blood.

Within this sequence, Campion signs her film in the cut between waking and dreaming, outside and inside, objective and subjective, present and past, both her own and that of her character. Mapped onto the visual ambivalences of the title sequence are allusions to her feature and early film work, the latter informing the visuals of Frannie's dream. The black, white, sepia, and red film stock of the dream sequence pointedly revisits the cinematography of *Mishaps: Seduction and Conquest*, while the ice skates and leather glove reanimate traumatic images from *A Girl's Own Story*, Campion's first sustained narrative (see photos pages 45 and 46). The title of either of these early shorts readily applies to the narrative of *In the Cut*, but more importantly, the dream renders Frannie's unconscious as deriving from the distant past of the filmmaker's

In the cut between waking and dream |

Fist in *In the Cut* |

student films, from an archeology of her early images and narrative techniques as she made the transition from artist to national industry-oriented filmmaker. In signing this credit sequence—whose content has no basis in the novel, but which derives from both Campion and Moore's earlier work—Campion signs the grafting, the generative cut of her own imagination onto that of Moore. The generic fatalism of Moore's novel is redirected to familial and artistic genealogies, to a present both haunted and inspired by the past.

Finally, the song "Que Será, Será" invokes the film genre's history and one of its most famous directors, having been written for Alfred Hitchcock's 1956 *The Man Who Knew Too Much*. Doris Day sang it as a lullaby to her character's son in that film and it later became wildly popular, its connection to the thriller forgotten. In addition to using an arrangement that, as David Denby notes, seems "neurotic—full of doubt" (112) to replace Day's "defiant" vocals, Campion disarticulates the song's narrative arc by moving the third verse, which begins, "When I grew up and fell in love, I asked my sweetheart, 'What lies ahead?'" to the end credits, the body of the film featuring first, second, and fourth verses wherein the singer daughter consults her mother, her teacher, and is then consulted by her own children when they ask her, "What will they be?" *In the Cut*'s opening sequence, however, ends with the second verse: "When I was just a child in school, I asked my teacher 'What shall I try? Should I paint pictures, should I sing songs?' Here was her wise reply—'Que será, será.'" In the context of Campion's film, this verse references *The Man Who Knew Too Much*'s concern with knowledge, but redirects it to women: to Frannie's profession and to a girl's destiny as involving education and a career as well as motherhood, these not necessarily involving the direction of one's "sweetheart." Also, in that the daughter's career questions to her teacher all have to do with the arts, the stanza is also self-referential to Campion's early film work, the questions about her future then in some ways answered by *In the Cut* and its revision of a Hitchcockian genre.

The end of the dream cuts to the beginning of the narrative proper—a shot of an apartment door, number ten. Just as the film ends with Frannie walking into and closing this door, so it begins with Pauline opening and walking out of it, Frannie right behind her. Pauline asks her the meaning of *virginia*, a slang word taped to her wall. Explaining that it means "vagina, as in, he penetrated her virginia with a hammer," Frannie notes that all slang refers to sex or violence. Pauline shudders and intones, "or both." Yet Frannie answers that she loves the wit and exuberance of slang. The novel and film's very title, *In the Cut*, exhibits this wit and exuberance *and* Pauline's "both," referring to the inside of a wound or gash (or the act that produces them) and to having sex, the vagina, and the birth canal (as in "We're born in the cut"). Campion works a third meaning into this vexed double "cut," her film crucially intervening in the mechanics of the thriller through its editing, through what it cuts from this genre's conventional visual repertoire.

Frannie's passion for language derives especially from its capacity to produce double meanings—in puns, onomatopoeia, poetry, and in slang where violence stands for and permeates sexual expression. Her simultaneous engagement with slang and poetry, with the base and the sublime, with double meanings that can go either way, provides a corollary for Campion's complicated genre experiment. In setting out to articulate a woman's point of view, her imagination, and her desire in a genre that depends for its pleasures on her death, Campion strategically incorporates fragments of poetry, literature by women, and melodramatic and romantic tropes that duplicate elements of the thriller, these duplications skewing or perverting ("to turn the wrong way") the dynamics of the "host" genre.

The film is littered with verbal, visual, and narrative examples of these duplications, from narrative props and events whose punning relationship invokes both crime and romance ("bracelets" refer both to handcuffs and women's wrist jewelry, here the courtship charm bracelet; Pauline literally "loses her head" to a man, a phrase often invoked to describe passionate love) to the tutor texts that Campion's *In the Cut* employs. Shortly after teaching her sister the meaning of *virginia*, Frannie is in the classroom, a blackboard drawing of a red lighthouse behind her, teaching her class Virginia Woolf's *To the Lighthouse*. One student remarks that the book is boring, "Nothing happens except an old lady dies." Frannie quips, "How many ladies have to die to make it interesting?" and, as the bell rings, another student calls out, "At least three." Campion takes this answer as her challenge. Three women *do* die in *In the Cut*, and Frannie actually travels to the lighthouse in the film's penultimate convergence of murder and romance (Rodriguez proposes marriage to all his victims before he kills them), literature and pop culture, sexuality and violence. Yet "nothing happens" in the conventional sense of this genre. The film does not generate suspense in the lead up to or the murders of any of the women, as Campion keeps these events off-screen. Instead of such generically graphic material, the film implements pictoral and verbal senses of the word "graphic." As one review notes, within "its density of visual imagery, *In the Cut* is also extraordinarily verbal," featuring numerous shots of written words in notebooks, on Post-its, on T-shirts, and on subway walls (Park and Dietrich, 44). Finally, *In the Cut* emphasizes the "graphic" doubling of sex/romance and violence without the usual industry cinema payoff—the externalizing and visualizing of this connection.

This doubling pervades the visual field as well. The thick rich shadows of noir appoint a color palette of browns, oranges, and reds above ground, whereas cool bluish tones prevail in the subway sequences. In her framings, Campion combines the necessary visual and narrative focus on her characters with strategies that provoke visual uncertainty and confusion. The shots are often thick with people, activity, and objects, the edges of the frame blurred and out of focus. At the level of cinematography and point of view, Campion generally eschews both omniscient perspectives and invisible style, instead employing a handheld camera and tight framings that suddenly shift back and forth to and from long shots in which our view is obstructed in some way or in which the source of the gaze is unclear. For example, as Frannie and Pauline step out onto the streets, arm in arm, we watch them in long shot through a café window, the camera situated indoors behind someone we cannot see who is watching them and gets up to follow them as they walk by. Following him following them, the camera then cuts in front of the two women, registering this shadowy, out-of-focus figure behind them as it also jerks to the side to become Cornelius's point of view, watching them from up ahead. Cutting close in to the two women, the camera then records an intimate exchange between them (about Cornelius "flirting" with Frannie), this shot sequence situating their intimacy in the cut between these two as yet unidentified and at least unsettling, if not hostile, male gazes.

This split and doubled point of view is typical of the film's many paranoid framings. Repeatedly, Frannie steps out on the street, our view of her coming through car windshields, the camera never revealing the source of these implicitly subjective gazes. Campion also uses windows and mirrors to generate multiple perspectives within a given sequence or shot, creating a miasmatic visual field that generates a persistent mood of apprehension, if not dread. Prettied up in Pauline's heels and dress, Frannie waits for Malloy, standing on a street corner in long shot, her image blurred. A cut to Malloy watching her registers that this blurred perspective is taken from the rearview mirror of his car. The camera then cuts to an objective view of her from the same distance, our gaze now complicit with his voyeurism, doubling his, both watching sadistically as she fidgets, checks her watch, looks for him. Only when she starts to walk away does the camera cut across the street, showing Malloy backing up his car, screeching to a stop in front of her. Earlier, when Frannie gets up from the table at her meeting with Cornelius, he tells her he has "bitch vision," the camera showing us his gaze as he looks her up and down. His "bitch vision" blends racialized erotics with affront, counters her authority (she is his teacher and older than him) with his desire. In these and other instances, the male gaze of industry cinema is variously objectified, differentiated, depersonalized, diffused, and multiplied throughout the mise-en-scène, becoming a continual, often anonymous surveillance, a hostile visual "thicket" that Frannie and Pauline move through.

But Frannie looks, too. After opening the door on the woman fellating the man, she lingers, watches, fascinated. When she masturbates after meeting Malloy, she fantasizes him watching her. Her gaze is explicitly contrasted with the male gaze in the sequence that crosscuts from a line of men watching the strippers in the bar downstairs from Pauline's apartment to Frannie reading Cornelius's paper about serial killer John Wayne Gacy upstairs. Whereas the multiple male gazes in the film seem to have only one object, Frannie's gaze has multiple objects. Her gaze is a reader's gaze, what she reads accessing her interiority, her imagination. Significantly, her voiceover narration is confined to telling her mother's story and, in the subway, to her recitation of the poetry of others, both associated with her unconscious and her imagination. As she rides the subway, we see her face, blank and still, as we hear her reading excerpts from the "Poetry in Transit" displayed in the cars. Surreal and dreamlike, these rides are appointed with iconic images that surface on the subway platforms: a five-foot-high heart-shaped arrangement of red carnations reading "Mom"; a bride in a long white dress whom Frannie watches out the window of her subway car as it slowly glides away. These sequences equate the icons with the words, as we see the lines of the poems in close-up as Frannie reads them, and then see them again as she rewrites them, copies them in her notebook, just as Campion rewrites the thriller, copies it in her own "writing" in this film.

At the same time Campion references literature and poetry through the passions and profession of her protagonist, she also "copies" from 1970s erotic thrillers from *Klute* (1971) to *Looking for Mr. Goodbar* (1977). These films featured female protagonists confronting the pleasures and dangers of their own sexuality in situations saturated with violence. Campion specifically cites the former film and *Taxi Driver* (1976) as inspirations, though her film bears an even more striking resemblance to *Looking for Mr. Goodbar.*[60] Frannie's relationship with Cornelius pointedly recalls Theresa's (Diane Keaton) with Cap Jackson (LeVar Burton), the older teenage brother of one of her deaf and mute first grade students. In each of these subplots, an older white woman misleads and confuses a younger black man with her attentions and intentions. This pairing pointedly inverts the stereotypical couple who form the representational cornerstone of American racism, the rapacious black man and the diminutive white girl/woman after whom he lusts.[61] Significantly, Frannie and Theresa's interracial and intergenerational flirting occurs in concert with their much more destructive, risk-taking sexual explorations with white men their own age. *In the Cut* thereby taps an alternative representational tradition that refers its treatment of dangerous female sexuality in the present to the 1970s emergence of such representations in the context of the feminist and civil rights movements. These movements claimed the rights of the disenfranchised to make their own choices, an assertion perversely reflected in *Goodbar*'s tale of a liberated woman and the fatally bad sexual choices she makes. At the same time, the film's interracial subplot implies that the black man is no longer a threat compared with the danger of a white woman's sexual choice—indeed, his threat was always predicated on her supposed lack of choice and desire. *In the Cut* revisits this scenario thirty years later, its view of white women's choices no longer reactionary, but resigned. Romance and sexuality are dangerous for such women—and in this instance the danger is entirely within their own race and class. Their desires and choices are insistently compromised by romantic myths whose fatality for women pointedly mirrors that of the thriller. *In the Cut* revises the latter genre and its mimicry of the romance by explicitly telling what are usually its backstories.

In place of the conventional actions, events, and plot of the thriller, *In the Cut* records signal stories told by its main characters. Frannie's story is her mother's story, recounted in three different narrative moments: the first as her dream that opens the film; the second as the courtship story that Frannie tells Pauline; and the third as a nightmare whose images apprehend Pauline's murder in the terms of Frannie's mother's courtship and heartbreak. In each instance, sepia-tinted black-and-white footage ruptures the narrative's otherwise realistic cinematography, representing Frannie's unconscious (in the first and third instances) and illustrating her story to Pauline in the second. Significantly, Frannie recounts "her mother's story" not from her own perspective or with her own words, but the way her mother "always told it." The mother's story consisted of how Frannie and Pauline's father proposed to Frannie's mother. He offered her the very engagement ring just thrown off by his former fiancée, enraged by the attentions he was paying to Frannie's mother. As Frannie recounts the story to Pauline, her words bridge the present, where the two women dance to Frannie's song—"Just My Imagination"—and the past, where we see the "imagined" skating scene of her parents' betrothal, her father, a dashing skater, going down on one knee to proffer the ring, "Que Será, Será" tinkling in the background. Frannie concludes by noting that this story "killed" her mother because when her father left, she couldn't believe it, couldn't understand.

Malloy tells a "teacher" and "student" story, his own story, from the past. When he and Frannie first have sex, he begins by going down on her, his proficiency clear from her ecstatic reactions. Pausing in their lovemaking, Frannie demands to know "how you did that to me," and suggests that "someone taught you." He admits he did have such a teacher, the "chicken lady," a housewife to whom he delivered groceries when he was fifteen. The woman seduced him, instructing him on everything he needed to know about sex, especially the finer points of cunnilingus. As Malloy recounts the chicken lady's actions and instructions to Frannie—"She wet her fingers"—he repeats, enacts them, wetting his fingers and performing his lesson on Frannie, this lesson leading to coitus. He has told Frannie, riffing on an earlier punning reference he made to Shakespeare's Hamlet ("Is that two *b*'s or not two *b*'s?") that he "can *be* whatever you want me to *be*." His teacher's story lives on in the present of the film, instigating narrative action and making Frannie the beneficiary of another woman's, another teacher's knowledge.

Unlike the other two, Pauline tells the story she is living in the wake of her mother's life. A married doctor with whom she had been having an affair has broken off their relationship and is pursuing a restraining order because Pauline has been stalking him and his wife (Pauline picked up a suit that his wife dropped off at the dry cleaners). On the evening before her court appearance, she tells Frannie that she thinks when the doctor sees her in court, he's going to realize that he's in love with her. They'll have a love child or two and then get married. She finishes by lamenting that even Angela Sands (the first murder victim) was engaged, to which Frannie responds that her fiancé probably cut off her head. Pauline has no visible profession, save romance. Infected by romantic fantasies completely at odds with reality, she wants to get married "just once" for her mother. Her fantasy brutally coincides with Rodriguez, a serial seducer/killer, and his story. He proposes and disposes, putting engagement rings on the fingers of each of his victims, an engagement ring on limbs that he later "disarticulates" from their bodies. Pauline finally "loses her head" to him, reliving Frannie's mother's betrothal story according to the dictates of a parallel genre.

Campion's films all deal, in one way or another, with stories and their power. They can kill or they can help us survive. Always interested in how the story is told as well as the story itself, she draws *In the Cut* from a wealth of stories and storytelling modes to find traces of a romantic story a woman might live by. Her sources range from Moore's novel to her own oeuvre, from industry cinema in its classical to New Hollywood era. The gambit of the song, "Que Será, Será," which plays in various forms throughout the film, is that of the life cycle, its passivity and fatalism directed toward daughter inevitably becoming mother. Although mother and teacher caution daughter/singer that "the future's not ours to see," the song itself mocks that assertion in the final verse, "Now I have children of my own, they ask their mother, what will they be?" In the song, the mother and her stories are both the past and the future, an endless repetition and duplication. Campion weds this genetic repetition to a generic one and, like Moore's protagonist, she "copies" the works of others.

In another possible homage to Hitchcock, Jane Campion signs *In the Cut* in a way she has not signed any of her other films—she makes an explicit on-screen appearance. In the bar scene where Frannie and Malloy meet for a drink, Campion, playing a barmaid, appears to the tune of "You're No Good," initially standing in front of a clock with no hands. She then takes a brief spin on the dance floor with Rodriguez, the man who, unbeknownst to us (on a first viewing at least), is the killer. He twirls her around, kisses her, and then rejoins the action. Here, Campion aligns herself with the film's killer, the disarticulator, the one who will kill off Pauline, associated with all her former films, and will be killed by Frannie, the one who shirks romance on its usual terms. Campion takes a spin, tells her tale, and then, in the last shot of the film, closes a door as the screen goes to black. In this film that she dedicates to her own daughter, she seeks to explore how the process of repeating and doubling can function as a "disarticulation" of romantic stories too fatal to relive.

Jane Campion on the dance floor |

Coda

In a conversation I had with Jane Campion, I asked her about the final-
ity and closure that seemed to be signaled by *In the Cut*'s ending. She
told me that she had not really thought about it and that she trusts her
unconscious and does not interrogate the images it produces. What I
have written here is my cut, my graft, my dance with Campion's images.
Her films have intrigued me because of their clear-eyed explorations of
violation and its aftermath without guilt or retribution; desire and will
in excess of reason; and wounding and its relation to power, healing,
and change. But what stays, what persists in a Campion film, beyond
narrative, are the images that, like Ada's will in *The Piano*, are so strange
and strong: a young girl with a Beatles mask practicing kissing with her
girlfriend; a sapling uprooted by a woman in the middle of the night, its
roots a ghostly echo of her legs in a diaphanous nightgown; jackaroos
dancing together under the stars in the outback; a woman, her skirts
high over her head, tethered underwater to her piano;[62] another woman,
trapped, her shoes confiscated, devising an escape from footwear made
out of ribbons and books. This last image is an apt visual metaphor for the

unwieldy and contradictory ingredients of feminine aspiration, mobility, and desire and with it, I will close.

Notes

1. The film swept the Australian Film Institute Awards in 1993, winning in all acting and technical categories as well as Best Picture and Director. It received either Best Picture or Best Director or both from the Independent Spirit Awards, the L.A. Film Critics, and the New York Film Critics. It won Academy Awards for Best Actress (Holly Hunter), Best Supporting Actress (Anna Paquin), and Best Screenplay. Internet Movie Database (www.imdb.com), *The Piano*, Awards.

2. B. Ruby Rich in conversation with Debbie Zimmerman at 2003 Toronto film festival.

3. For a discussion of the heated debates over whether *The Piano* was an Australian or a New Zealand film and whether Campion was an Australian or New Zealand filmmaker, see Pihama, "Ebony and Ivory," 114–16.

4. Many scholars of surrealism claim Kahlo for their school—one even naming a book on surrealism and women *The Beribboned Bomb* from Andre Breton's comment that "the art of Frida Kahlo is a ribbon about a bomb." Kahlo herself sometimes accepted such nominations, sometimes rejected them, and rather than identifying herself as surrealist, instead discussed her uses of surrealism. Diego Rivera insisted she was a realist. See Herrera, 214, 254–64.

5. Described in Robson and Zalcock as "the first major [Australian] film to be directed by a woman in over forty years" (9).

6. In 1983, AFTRS's incoming class included eight women, and in Campion's last year at AFTRS, the school instituted an on-the-job training program for women. AFTRS Web site—"About AFTRS." Aftrs.edu.au/90.cfm. In 1995, 50% of all the funding granted by the Australian Film Commission went to women filmmakers (Robson and Zalcock 3). See also Barbara Alysen, "Australian Women in Film," and Leslie Stern's "Independent Feminist Film-making in Australia" in Moran and O'Regan.

7. See Robson and Zalcock, 41–42; Puskin, 210; and Polan, 55.

8. See Noel King and Toby Miller's extremely useful summary of the issues in "Auteurism in the 1990s."

9. Thanks to Felicity Nussbaum for her invaluable insights and feedback on my readings of Campion's early films, here for how Campion foregrounds women's self-destructive behaviors. I am indebted to Richard Yarborough for suggesting that I take a closer look at Campion's representations of masculinity in *The Piano*, a suggestion that enhanced the overall project. On Campion's representation of children, see Modleski's "Axe the Piano Player."

10. Having read many of George Mallory's letters to his wife, among others, it seems to me that Campion simulated Mallory's writing style in the letters she

wrote that form the backbone of this film's script without ever directly citing them.

11. Similarly, George Mallory's relation to his will seems very similar to Ada's relation to hers: on more than one occasion, she speaks, as he did, of being afraid of her own will, of what it might cause her to do.

12. On his expeditions to Everest, Mallory would stride around the lower altitudes naked, as is documented in a photograph included in David Breashears and Audrey Salkeld's *Last Climb*, 83. He was reputedly fearless and also quite absentminded: "On several expeditions he would take photos at the summit only to find later that he had left the lens cap on his camera." On his last, fatal ascent of Everest's summit, Mallory forgot to pack a flashlight and flares, the latter of which might have saved his life and possibly that of his companion, Andrew Irvine. On his relationship to Bloomsbury, see Anker and Roberts, "Mon Dieu! George Mallory." An article in *The Week*, 8 May 1999, details his absentmindedness. http://elt.britcoun.org.pl/s_mallor.htm

13. I am limiting my analysis in this book to Campion's theatrically released features and will not discuss the work she did for television—*After Hours* (1984), *Dancing Daze* (1985), and *Two Friends* (1986)—in the interim between film school and the theatrical release of *Sweetie*. I discuss female narration in Campion's feature films in McHugh, 2001.

14. See Laleen Jayamanne's discussion of mimetic contagion in "Postcolonial Gothic."

15. Many people invoke Lacan's ideas in discussing Campion's work, particularly *The Piano*, and with good reason, as Lacan was heavily influenced by the surrealists, particularly Roger Caillois and his theories of mimicry. Surrealism was, in turn, influenced by Freud. Yet because of Campion's training in the arts and her association with surrealism, I have chosen to discuss her work in relation to this visual aesthetic rather than the Lacanian psychoanalytic theory derived from it.

16. Writers and reviewers who explicitly label the film "feminist" are far too numerous to detail here, but some excellent examples and resources include Stella Bruzzi (257), Pam Cook (xii–xiv), Carol Jacobs (758), and Harriet Margolis (26). Margolis also includes citations for articles written about the arguments generated by the film (32n4). Sue Gillett's essay discusses and cites reviews that argue Campion's film represents a woman falling in love with her rapist ("Lips and Fingers" 282). She also mentions that when she delivers talks on *The Piano*, audience members frequently argue that both Stewart and Baines are rapists (282). See also Carolyn Gage (54).

17. Such a politics would strive to articulate a different relationship between the present and the past, a relationship that Wendy Brown also draws from Nietzsche. Nietzsche warns against a perspective dominated by "it was," a perspective that leaves the will "powerless against what has been done, [. . .] an angry spectator of all that is past." The power of the past must be reduced "by remaking the present against the terms of the past—in short, by a project of

self-transformation that arrays itself against its own genealogical consciousness" (Brown 72). This type of transformation might well make use of aesthetics and different modes of historicizing and storytelling.

18. Anneke Smelik's astute discussion of *Sweetie* considers its use of magical thinking from a psychoanalytic perspective and the doubling of the sisters in relation to the gothic. See "Forces of Subversion: On the Excess of the Image," in *And the Mirror Cracked*.

19. Writers on surrealism, such as Hal Foster, associate objective chance with trauma, arguing that it is a structure wherein "the anxious is projected as the portentous" (29–30).

20. Though it is certainly true, as Geraldine Bloustien asserts, that "music in all Campion's films is closely linked to personal dreams and fantasies" (7), Campion uses compelling music in such a way that it objectifies those fantasies. As spectators, we don't share them, we examine them.

21. "Baby elder," a term that aptly describes Sweetie, Kay, and Gordon, also serves as a metaphor for the traumatized child within the adult.

22. In addition to observing *Sweetie*'s astute rendering of trauma, Gillett also notes, without naming it as such, the film's ethnographic acuity: "this is a film which seems to 'know' . . . what it was like growing up female and working class, in Australia in the '60s, in a family where husbands are sons to their wives, and daughters are wives to their fathers, where mothers and daughters are rivals and the father a destructive child" ("More than," 6).

23. Critics and reviewers attribute the film's look to Sally Bongers's cinematography. See Hinsen, Howe, Polan, Smelik, Woodard.

24. Frame's *To the Is-Land* was published in 1982 during Campion's second year in film school. *An Angel at My Table* followed in 1984, and then *An Envoy from Mirror City* was published in 1985.

25. The film cost $2,710,00 to make and grossed $4,784,670. FRCE report.

26. Jane's sister Anna Campion made a short film, called *The Audition*, of Edith Campion trying out for this part.

27. Polan connects these performances to class and to Janet's learning to fictionalize (112–13).

28. In Frame's last year in high school, she won a speech prize and her father gave her five shillings that she used to purchase the first book she ever bought, *Lavengro*, by George Borrow. It contained this passage. Several years after making the film, Campion named her infant son, who only survived for twelve days, Jasper (Frame 124).

29. Tara Hawes, writing on Frame's *An Autobiography*, sees Frame only becoming a "third person" when she is institutionalized, but Frame herself clearly identified childhood as a state of "third person" (4).

30. In "Angel from the Mirror City," Sue Gillett discusses Campion's novel cinematic representation of the female body "in terms of how it is experienced

and inhabited . . . in relation to menstruation, pregnancy, and miscarriage" (12). See also Henke's discussion of Janet's menstrual issues (657–58).

31. For an essay that focuses on the palpably tactile quality of this film, see Vivian Sobchack, "What My Fingers Knew: The Cinesthetic Subject, or Vision in the Flesh."

32. The problem of women's speech runs throughout Campion's films and aligns them with art/auteur cinema of the 1950s and 60s, a cinema she knew well. In Akira Kurosawa's *Rashomon* (1950), the wife, Masago (Machiko Kyo), says, "How can I, a woman, speak?"—her question underscoring that she has no ability, no standing to make a choice. Ada's muteness recalls that of Elizabeth (Liv Ulmann) in Ingmar Bergman's *Persona,* a woman who inexplicably withdraws into silence. As I will discuss below, Campion is also drawing from the muteness endemic to women in industry film melodrama.

33. Carol Jacobs observes that Ada's will "is strangely disconnected from conventional concepts of volition [. . .,] a will, then, that is like a passion outside the realm of tame self-interest and self-knowledge" (771).

34. For example, Ada's father marries Ada to Stewart; Stewart trades Ada's piano to Baines for land; Stewart attempts to trade blankets and guns to Maoris for their sacred burial land; he trades buttons for their labor; Baines trades Ada and Ada trades Baines piano keys for sexual favors; Stewart and the narrative exchange Ada's piano key with its declaration of love for her finger.

35. Leonie Pihama exemplifies the critical perspective of the film's depiction of the Maori. Margolis's introduction to *Jane Campion's The Piano* includes a valuable discussion of the debates that took place in New Zealand on this issue (15–24).

36. For example, Dyson critiques the film as relegating the Maoris to the background and associating them with nature to the European colonials' culture. She and Reid assert that a black/white binary structures the film. Anna Neill argues that the film aligns colonial oppression with patriarchal oppression, then has the "Maori culture" facilitate the articulation of a "white post-colonial subject" (140). Orr asserts that the white man's colonial culpability and the film's metonymic association of Ada and the Maori exempts her from colonial responsibility.

37. Neill critiques Campion by deliberately misreading her. She uses this quote from Campion: "I think it is a strange heritage that I have as a *Pakeha* New Zealander, and I want to be in a position to explore that. In contrast to the original people in New Zealand, the Maori people . . . we seem to have no history or . . . tradition. This makes you ask 'Well, who are my ancestors?' My ancestors are the English colonizers." She then, incredibly, interprets the director as saying that "being a *Pakeha* New Zealander, [Campion] seems to suggest, is not quite the same thing as being the descendent of an English colonizer" (141).

38. The mute heroine in Janet Frame's *Scented Gardens for the Blind* bears mention here as well.

39. See Simmons on this motif in New Zealand landscape painting.

40. The shot of Ada's piano on the beach, huge waves breaking in the background, is explicitly coded as her imagination. Set against this highly romanticized image are: the Maori's material and historically precise appropriations of European dress (an image that challenges many critics' assertions that the film relegates the Maori to a mythic prehistory before time—ergo before European contact); colonial women and girls vomiting, urinating, and sinking knee deep in the mud, the extreme incongruity and inappropriateness of their dress thereby dramatically underscored and deromanticized. See Bruzzi.

41. Joannes Fabian's *Time and the Other* describes how this process takes place through the discourse of anthropology, one that provided "the intellectual justification of the colonial enterprise" (17–18).

42. For a thorough historical and theoretical account of the tea trade and its manifold exploitations and ironies, see Piya Chatterjee's *A Time for Tea: Women, Labor and Post-Colonial Politics on an Indian Plantation*.

43. See Jayamanne's discussion of mimesis in this film, 39–46.

44. See Caroline Molina on the aesthetics of disability in this film.

45. Margaroni asserts that all holders of gaze in the film are ultimately disempowered (106).

46. For two excellent articles that deal extensively with Flora's character, see Modleski and Margaroni.

47. Wexman discusses the similarities between Ada and Isabel in "Portrait of a Body," stressing Campion's overall emphasis on physicality in her films, 186.

48. Nancy Bentley, in "Conscious Observation of a Lovely Woman," writes, "When I saw the film, more than one viewer in the audience, no doubt remembering Campion's film *The Piano*, gasped when Isabel declared, 'I would give my little finger'" (178). See also Virginia Wexman's discussion in "The Portrait of a Body" (185).

49. Many critics of the film see this image as incestuous. See Bauer, 195.

50. Gordon argues that Campion represents Osmond as literally hypnotizing, mesmerizing Isabel (18).

51. Her total budget for this film, including production and advertising costs, was $36,791,000, $13 million more than her second-most-expensive film, *In the Cut*, and three times the budget of the third, *The Piano*.

52. Industry examples include: *A Room with a View* (1985), *Howard's End* (1992), *Emma* (1996), and *Sense and Sensibility* (1995). Feminist independent titles are: *Orlando* (1993) by Potter, and *Mansfield Park* (1999) by Rozema. *Clueless*, Amy Heckerling's witty 1995 adaptation of Austen's *Emma*, is an example of that rare anomaly, a feminist industry film.

53. To create this "Indian vision," the VFX cinematographer referenced Bol-

lywood film and its movie posters to create "a kaleidoscope of metaphors" blending East and West (Brown 2).

54. Campion's narrative implicitly brings together three former colonies of Britain, juxtaposing them in variable relations of power and empire: the United States, former British colony, represents empire to Australia; Australia, former British colony, represents empire to India.

55. Conversation with Piya Chatterjee about *Holy Smoke*, September 23, 2000.

56. Campion's use of a 1950s/'60s girl group, the Shirelles, to accompany film footage of a deity also recalls Kenneth Anger's similar juxtapositions of girl groups with Hollywood images of Christ in his avant-garde exploration of gay sexuality and fetishism, in *Scorpio Rising* (1963).

57. See Linda Ruth Williams's discussion of *In the Cut*'s feminist take on the erotic thriller genre, including its remarkable blow job scene, which inverts the erotic objectification of women's bodies by featuring a close-up of an (albeit prosthetic) erection (418–20).

58. "James's side of the square" alludes to the location of the Sloper residence in his story *Washington Square*, adapted by Hollywood in 1949 as *The Heiress* and again, in 1997, as *Washington Square,* with Jennifer Jason Leigh playing Catherine, another daughter of a very problematic father.

59. The score was done by Pink Martini. The song's title, "Que Será, Será (Whatever Will Be Will Be)" reflects the answer to life's questions as posed in the lyrics. The singer recalls asking her mother whether she would be pretty and rich; her teacher, what she should attempt; her sweetheart, what lies ahead. Her children, in turn, ask her the same questions. Significantly, the version made famous by Doris Day omitted the teacher verse.

60. Thanks to Richard Yarborough for suggesting I take a look at *Looking for Mr. Goodbar* in relation to Campion's film. See also Linda Ruth Williams, 419.

61. See Linda Williams's extended discussion of the significance of this stereotypical couple in American popular culture in *Playing the Race Card*.

62. See Barbara Klinger's compelling discussion of this as an "arresting image" in "The Art Film, Affect, and the Female Viewer: *The Piano* Revisited," 19–41.

interviews with Jane Campion
Michel Ciment

These two encounters with Jane Campion took place three years apart from each other. The first was in Paris a few months after the presentation of her shorts at the Cannes Film Festival 1986. The second was in Cannes last year after the projection of *Sweetie*, which confirmed her immense talent.

Short and Medium-Length Films

MC: What was the idea behind your first film *Peel*?

JC: I knew a family which was extremely unusual, and I thought it would be interesting to film them. They were people who didn't seem to be able to control themselves. I would suggest scenes for them, and since they were very honest, they realized that they revealed their true nature in these scenes. It's a very short film of about nine minutes.

MC: *Passionless Moments* was more elaborate.

JC: It was the result of collaboration with one of my friends, Gerard

Lee. It was his idea at the beginning and we wrote and directed the film together. Once we had the frame of the film—a series of playlets—we tried to imagine the maximum number of stories that would be told with a certain ironic distance. We finally wrote ten of them. Gerard and I wanted to show sweet, ordinary people that you rarely see on screen and who have more charm than better-known actors. The film was shot in five days, two episodes per day. I was also responsible for the photography and I realized the benefit of film school where in two hours I had learned how to light and to exploit the possibilities of the camera.

MC: All these short films have in common the sense of observation, the choice of moments, of epiphanies where behaviors reveal themselves.

JC: That always interested me. I remember that at film school my classmates wanted to make big movies or spectacular scenes with car crashes. That was the last thing I wanted to do.

MC: You love Katherine Mansfield, your countrywoman, who was also interested in the observation of details?

JC: Yes. I love her books. When I was a child in New Zealand, I played next to her monument which was in a park near our house.

MC: To what extent is *A Girl's Own Story* inspired by your childhood and adolescence?

JC: I wanted to pay homage to that period of our lives when we feel lost and alone. It's very characteristic of youth. It's a very curious stage in our development where we feel adult emotions but we lack experience. With experience it's easier to face our emotions. The smallest things seem immense obstacles when you're very young. I had lived many experiences that I had never seen represented. For example, in class everybody kissed each other and as soon as we grew up we stopped doing it. I also wanted to talk about the Beatles whose music touched my generation since I was born in 1954. The episode of incest wasn't a personal experience but I remember a very young neighbor who got pregnant by a classmate and the scandal that it created.

MC: Did the actors bring you the material or was everything written from the start?

JC: Of course, the actors always contribute a little. But in this particular case the adolescents thought I was very bizarre and swore they had never done anything similar. In fact, they essentially recited the text. I had a hard time finding the actors. The first one I chose did not feel at all at ease with the incest. She was too immature and I had to get someone older but who appeared younger than her age. The shooting officially ran ten days, but I was able to "steal" extra time. The whole crew was formed by students and we didn't have a lot of experience but the film was well received in Australia and even won some prizes. When it was shown in theaters, the reaction was very good, people laughed a lot, so much that it was hard to hear the dialogue. That moved me because my professors had never supported my work. They were conservative people who thought that type of film was too strange to allow me to get a job.

MC: It was after leaving school that you made *After Hours*.

JC: Yes. On the basis of my short films, the Women's Film Unit suggested that I write and make this film. I don't like *After Hours* a lot because I feel like the reasons for making it were impure. I felt a conflict between the project and my artistic conscience. The film, commissioned by Women Production Unity, had to be openly feminist since it spoke about the sexual abuse of women at work. I wasn't comfortable because I don't like films that say how one should or shouldn't behave. I think that the world is more complicated than that. I prefer watching people, studying their behavior without blaming them. I would have preferred to have put this film in a closet but it toured the world! I like making movies that I would like to see as a spectator and that's not the case with *After Hours*, but it was important for me to do it.

MC: You then made an episode of *Dancing Daze* for ABC.

JC: It was a commission, light entertainment for television. I was in the process of writing a project for television series on the New Zealander writer Janet Frame and I wanted to know what it was like to work for television. It was an interesting experience, even though I don't care much for the film. However, it allowed me to meet Jan Chapman, who later produced *Two Friends*. I was obliged to work fast and to make a fifty-minute film in seven days with song and dance numbers. It was the classic story of a group of young people who, in 1986, want to make a dance troupe. I had to be visually inventive, which amused me and gave me confidence that I could do commercial films.

MC: A little later you made *Two Friends*.

JC: It had to be quick, because ABC had a crew available and an opening in their production plan. The preparation was short. Helen

Gardner's screenplay was proposed to me by, as I told you, the producer Jan Chapman. We agreed on objectives and we had relationship of trust. I also liked the script a lot, even if the idea of telling a story by going back in time was not what I would have chosen. What I loved was the freshness of observation and the truth of situations. I felt I could get something out of it. Helen Gardner had been inspired by the experiences of her daughter and one of her friends. I went to Melbourne to meet them. The student who played the role of the daughter had blond hair and we thought she wasn't serious enough. We gave her brown hair and cut it like a boy's. I think that on the whole it's not too difficult to work with adolescents even if there are certain days when their emotions are very confused.

MC: How do objects, which are numerous in your films, help the actors in their work?

JC: I like first to observe what they do normally in life and I remind them of it when we shoot so that their acting is natural, comes from real-life experience.

MC: Do you often oversee the camerawork?

JC: I like to look in the viewfinder because I am very precise about the frame that I want. During the shooting of *Two Friends*, the crew under the director of photography felt some resentment towards me because they weren't used to a director who deals with things like that. My director of photography didn't understand what I wanted very well and I had to be very obstinate to impose my views. On the other hand, with Sally Bongers, a friend who studied with me and who also shot *Peel* and *A Girl's Own Story*, I had a very good relationship. For *Two Friends*, by contrast, I had to use the television crew. They were very competent, but we very simply had different methods of shooting.

MC: Do you do a lot of takes?

JC: No. For *Two Friends* for example we decided on a visual style. We knew that there would be close-ups, and as soon as the actors played the scene with the right tone we went on to the next shot. I didn't thus "cover" myself. It was a very economical shoot on the whole.

MC: Do you plan to continue to focus in on intimate stories?

JC: I hope that there will always be the same sense of observation in my films since I think that it's a strength, but I'm not sure that my stories will stay intimate. I have a big desire to work on a larger scale with more powerful stories, different materials. I'm presently working on a project that comes close to the spirit and the atmosphere of a Grimm's fairy tale. It's a love story situated in New Zealand around 1850 with a rather dark tone.

MC: Did you choose to portray youth in *A Girl's Own Story* and *Two Friends* because it was reassuring for you in your first work to deal with themes that were familiar to you?

JC: In the case of *A Girl's Own Story*, I had a desire to explore a universe that I knew well. I also like young people very much: I think they're free and generous with themselves. But it's not an obsession on my part! Of course, now whenever someone writes a story with young girls in it, they think of me to make a movie out of it. But each generation interests me. In fact I would like to tell all sorts of stories. I'm currently rereading *Treasure Island* and I'm getting a lot of pleasure out of it. I like its force, its audacity, but also its sense of observation. In any case, I always remember to maintain a certain irony.

Sweetie

MC: What have you done in the three years that separate your short films from *Sweetie*?

JC: After the screening of my films at the Cannes Film Festival, I thought about what I was going to take on given that some possibilities opened up for me. The first project that I wanted very much to do was *Sweetie* because it seemed to be based on the most modern and provocative point of view. Moreover, it was financially doable. I also thought that after a more "serious" film it would be difficult to make *Sweetie*! I have a provocative side and I was very happy to take on this subject. I began to develop this story with my co-screenwriter Gerard Lee, the friend who had already written *Passionless Moments* with me and who is someone who is very intelligent. It was a topic that he was very familiar with, that belonged to both of us, and we were on the same wavelength. It took me three years to make *Sweetie* because during that period I also developed other projects. One was *The Piano,* a very romantic story in the tone of the Brontë sisters that I would like to make later. I also worked on *Janet Frame* which will be my next film. This will be a portrait of a New Zealand author who wrote various autobiographical volumes which revolve around what it means to grow up and what it means to create. I love the style of her autobiographical trilogy: *To the Island,* which concerns her childhood, is full of freshness and is the most seductive of the three. *An Angel at My Table* and *An Envoy to Mirror City* include many events that take place in Europe. It's for that that I recently made some trips to your continent to scout locations. I will shoot it for television in three one-hour parts with the possibility of making a film version.

MC: Did you have difficulty in financing *Sweetie?*

JC: Finding money to write these three projects was not difficult. As for the production of *Sweetie,* it was done without too many problems since the film was very cheap, less than a million dollars. The screenplay was written with this in mind. It had been inspired by people and events that I was familiar with. I always work like that. It gives me more confidence to write and even if I then stray from these experiences, I always have a base which I can go back to. The character of *Sweetie* was inspired by a man, but for family reasons we changed gender. That was disappointing to me at the beginning, but I respected the feelings of my co-screenwriter. What I loved about *Sweetie* was the potential there was in her and the way in which it crumbled. That happens to all of us. One day we explore what we could be, then that day passes and it's too late. It's a poignant character with hope.

MC: In one sense Kay is the central character. The others join in the story progressively, first Louis, then Sweetie, then her parents.

JC: We called the film *Sweetie* because it was a pretty title, not because she's the heroine of the story. Kay evolves, she feels more courageous. I also believe that you cannot love without having a real base; otherwise you only love an illusion and that doesn't work. But most of us somehow create illusions around what we do. We have an idea in our head of what our partner is like and the fact that they are different from this idea is hard to accept.

MC: Did you always have the idea of beginning with the voice-over what's going on in Kay's head?

JC: No. In the beginning I thought I would start with some shots of trees. They were beautiful shots but I thought that that would disorientate the audience, that they had too many elements to put together. At the same time, when I make movies, I have the impression that I can do anything, that I am completely free as long as it contributes to the story, as long as it makes sense. I like things to be fresh and surprising. With Kay's voice-over, we wanted to indicate from the start that we weren't only interested in what the characters do but also in what they think and feel.

MC: In what part of Australia does the action take place?

JC: Essentially in Willoughby, a suburb north of Sydney. The scenes where they go visit their mother were shot in Warren in the northwest of South Wales, a fantastic city, a cotton-growing and sheep-raising center. I loved shooting there. We trampled the earth to give it the arid, desert-like look of certain regions of Australia where we didn't have the means to shoot.

MC: In Kafka's *The Metamorphosis*, all is seen from the point of view of the "abnormal" son. Here it's more the view of the family who are faced with Sweetie's otherness.

JC: I thought however that from time to time it would be good to hear what Sweetie thinks or feels, like the moment when the family leaves to go west and where, by her reaction, you understand what a baby she is. Her father is a traitor and a bastard who creates hope in vain. He knows that if he takes Sweetie away he can never bring his wife back. I remember that the actor who played the part of Gordon had the same reactions as his character; he really felt in a fix at that time!

MC: Your frames are stunning. Are they preplanned or are you inspired by the filming?

JC: I had nothing to lose, it was a small budget and we could be audacious, take some risks. We were shooting for our own pleasure. Many things were spelled out ahead of time. Sally Bongers, my cinematographer, thinks like me. We talk a lot, drink tea, laugh, imagine shots, look around us to borrow things. We are both very visually oriented and our aesthetic senses are very close. Sally also has a lot of good sense regarding scenes; she frames to highlight the dramatic situation and the emotions involved but she's also careful not to attract too much of the audience's attention to the photography! We made some mistakes of this kind. In certain scenes you don't feel as if the characters are speaking to each other since they were on opposite sides of the frame! We had to reshoot them. I am good friends with Sally Bongers which doesn't prevent us from arguing because of the control that each of us wants to exert. She is very stubborn, very strong, and sometimes wants certain things. And since I resemble her, and I sometimes have opposing ideas, conflict is inevitable! They aren't really disagreements, but the result of the pressures that filming produce.

As for the lighting, Sally was essentially responsible and she was very intuitive. But we discussed it ahead of time and we wanted soft light on the faces since that's what we felt towards the characters. In the beginning I was afraid that the shots would seem pretentious, but I no longer have that horrible feeling. What I wanted was to cross the line that allows a shot to create the emotional aspect of a situation, as in photography, which is a much more adventurous art than film from this point of view. There is a sensibility, a sophistication in photography that I often don't find in film and I would like to continue to tackle this visual research and story development.

An Interview with Jane Campion
Judith Lewis

Wholly Jane

"Did you read *The Journalist and the Murderer*?" Jane Campion asks a few minutes into our conversation, invoking Janet Malcolm's definitive exposé of how journalists exploit the people they write about. "Pretty neat, that book. Very smart writer. I *love* her." It is, I agree, a marvelous book, whose story—of a biographer who curries favor with his alleged-murderer subject only to turn on him in the end—no respectable writer of profiles could fail to be profoundly affected by. But I can't see what it has to do with Campion and me, sitting in the lobby bar of the Beverly Hills adjacent Four Seasons, chatting about her new film, *Holy Smoke*. "Well," Campion suggests, "we're playing that out right now, don't you think?"

To be wary about the process is perhaps Campion's right after a long day of interviews. (Lest I forget she's had one, Harvey Keitel stops by: "Jane," he says in the sort of hushed tone that's impossible to ignore, "if we ever do another film together, I'm going to make it my last film, because I'll never do another interview again—which means I'll never *work* again.") Still, I try to object: Campion is, after all, a filmmaker, not a criminal, and I am, after all, an exceedingly friendly witness who counts herself among the women who regard her films, *An Angel at My Table* and *The Piano* in particular, with the same esteem Campion holds for the novels of George Eliot and Charlotte Brontë. ("They validate me," she says.)

But she persists. "That's how it goes, you know—in the beginning you're kind of chuffed that people are interested in you, and you believe it. It's all so simple, really, so childish: Very simply and babyishly you trust them all and you say things thinking it all sounds so cute. And then," she says, "you read it."

With that, she laughs: The large, long, raucous laugh other people have written about before, most of them offering various interpretations of its function: nervousness, control, diversion, emotional masking. (One British journalist went so far as to label it "hysterical," unaware, perhaps, of that word's particularly rich etymology.) The temptation is to offer another analysis—to assert that, just as Campion's characters negotiate the mined terrain of seduction and power, hers is a seductive and powerful laugh. But it also comes from her gut and takes over her face, which despite its patrician cheekbones and blue-eyed beauty conveys an unguardedness that makes you feel safe divulging secrets. So here's another theory: Jane Campion just really likes to laugh.

She is no more capable of suppressing that laugh than she is of concealing her opinion. On the other hand, "I'm an idiot," she says, "because as soon as I say something I think I can stick with, I immediately realize that the opposite is true." Which helps to explain why *Holy Smoke* so stubbornly refuses to yield any lessons in ethics. The story of a young Australian woman named Ruth (played by Kate Winslet), whose parents attempt to "rescue" her from a Hindu religious community they believe is a cult, *Holy Smoke* neither endorses nor indicts. The spiritual community that captivates Ruth may seem patriarchal and controlling, what with its charismatic "Baba" luring young women with his mesmerizing stare, but Ruth's family is certainly no better, nor is the adviser, P. J. (Keitel), to whom her mother and father deliver her for "deprogramming."

"I'm not saying she isn't involved in a cult," says Campion, who in the course of researching the film heard both sides of the story—gurus who transformed lives for the better and cults who tried to break their acolytes' wills. "I'm not sure. But I'm not sitting in judgment of any of them, because I do think that everybody has to address the situation of their spirit in their own time, and try to find some inspiration to follow, something to lead you. Some people do it by joining a very full-on religion, and they get lost in it, and some people do the same thing and just use it for what it's worth. What the film tries to say is that there isn't a simple solution to it. It's like a relationship—you don't just find the perfect person and then off you go. It's something you're going to be working on for the rest of your life. And you may find inspiration from different sources as well."

Campion herself finds inspiration in unexpected places, and the real-life stories she cites as muses do not always match up with what you think you saw onscreen. The strange and morally ambiguous relationship that evolves between Ruth and P. J., for instance, is based in part on a two- or three-night romance she had with a much younger man. "He had cystic fibrosis," she tells me, "and I knew he wasn't going to live very long." The laugh subsides and she goes quiet. "He was one of the most courageous people I ever met."

"Sometimes you get touched by someone's spirit and it helps you identify a different path in life that you never forget," she continues. "It's one of those situations almost everyone has at some point, in which someone showed you some love and you didn't acknowledge it at the time, and you think about what courage it took for that person to do that, and you're ashamed that you missed it. It kind of haunts you." I assume she's talking about Ruth's love. But no. "P. J.," says Campion, "is probably the first man who ever loved Ruth." Considering that what P. J. does to Ruth may in most company qualify as flat-out abuse, that's at least a complicated statement. Simplicity, of course, is rarely the hallmark of a great filmmaker.

The unruly women about whom Campion makes movies are not easy to fit into any ideological framework: sometimes they're crushed by their own willfulness; other times, they "choose life," as Holly Hunter's Ada put it in *The Piano*, and emerge whole. If they are avatars of feminism, it is a feminism that Campion finds impossible to articulate. "The laws of men and women in Western society are carefully unwritten," she says. "And feeling them, facing up to them, is like the pain of having a baby—no one will ever tell you about it, really, because it's just beyond communicating. It's so bad, so big, so enormous, that you can't describe it or even believe it. In a way it's the same for women feeling the world, facing the world. I don't even talk about it, because it sounds like whinge-ing. But I'm not whingeing. I'm screaming."

Which is to be distinguished from complaining. "I love being a woman," she affirms. "It's a pretty good role, really, like being in the background of an amazing painting. The background isn't being focused on, so it's a good time; you have more freedom, you don't have to sit still, you're less examined. You don't have the responsibilities that you have in the foreground, responsibilities that can numb you creatively. A guy is told, 'You have to earn a living.' That's a life sentence of its own, and I would think that could be really horrible. I was told, 'You'll never have to earn a living—you'll never be able to, so don't even think about it.' There's a freedom in that."

And yet as much as she loves men—and she explicitly does—she doubts she'll ever make a movie with a man at its center. "I was going to do one about Christopher Isherwood and his guru [Swami Prabhava-nanda], the one who chain-smoked and wore pointy shoes, but I couldn't get the script right. Isherwood being a gay artist—I guess that's as close as I'll get." Her next film, an adaptation of Susanna Moore's erotic thriller *In the Cut*, she's coproducing with Lori Parker and Nicole Kidman, who will also star. "I like to be able to project myself into the parts," says Campion, "and being a woman I like to therefore have heroines. We don't have many, you know? So I feel like it's my job. Not a crusade—just a natural thing to want to do."

An Interview with Jane Campion |
Lizzie Francke

Dangerous Liaisons

LIZZIE FRANCKE: *In the Cut*, much like *The Piano* and *The Portrait of a Lady*, deals with female masochism.

JANE CAMPION: I think I relate to emotional masochism rather than physical because I hate to hurt myself or to see someone else hurting themselves. Susanna Moore's book is quite nihilistic and deals directly with female self-sacrifice—even when she's dying (which she does in the book), the lead character Frannie is imagining how her male killer would see her, wondering if he'd notice she'd scratched him and his flesh is under her fingernails. In our culture, male ideas so dominate our psyches we tend to think of ourselves through a male screen. It's inherent in the myths of romance and love we live with—if you haven't got a man loving you or you're not in a relationship it's as if you're not alive, as if what happens to you has no value.

LF: Is there a positive path through these myths?

JC: The positive thing about the story is that there's a redemptive quality at the end. Frannie has worked her way towards a stripped-down, truthful relationship with Detective Malloy. I think in this story, sex and the body are where truth lies, and Frannie feels instinctively, from the way Malloy makes love, that he can't be the murderer because he's a man who likes women. When he says to her, "There isn't very much I haven't done, so what do you want? Do you want me to romance you, take you to classy restaurants? Do you want me to lick your pussy?" he's cutting right through and it's shocking to her. They are both truth-lovers: people such as Frannie who love poetry are truth-seekers, and detectives are too. And what's also attractive to Frannie is that Malloy operates at street level. Having removed herself further and further from real life, she recognizes that the perfect person to bring her back is someone who can confront the worst aspects of society and is trying to clean up the mess.

LF: You could see Malloy as a double of the killer.

JC: I didn't think of it that way—it was more interesting to me to look at how someone can distort romantic ideals to the extent the murderer does. Robert Browning wrote a poem called "Porphyria's Lover" in which he describes strangling your lover as an ideal situation because then you can arrange them any way you like, and know they're not going to answer back. Here, because the murderer's way of killing is romantically inspired, the girls reconsider the myths they've been disappointed by—sex, marriage, and commitment—and these elements become woven into the story.

LF: What about the vignette of the tale of Frannie's mother?

JC: I thought we were going to chuck that out as we were filming it, but it works really well. One of the things that surprised me when I was putting together the film was the scene when Frannie's dancing with her half-sister Pauline and recounting the romantic story of how her father proposed to her mother, whom he later abandoned. It's Frannie revealing the whole reason why she's so skeptical.

LF: You seem to be developing a riposte to existing gender mythologies.

JC: I enjoyed making this film because I got the opportunity to read a lot of poems and to think about love, romance, and sex and how they've infested people's psyches. And it's not often you see sex on screen that's designed to be pleasurable for the woman.

LF: Meg Ryan reinvents herself as an actress to play Frannie, much as Nicole Kidman did in *The Portrait of a Lady*. Is it important for you to find new aspects to your actors?

JC: I think Nicole had got stuck in a string of bad Hollywood movies that were depressing her, and Meg felt the same. She'd started getting acting coaching, and a coach called Sandra Secat called me and said I should audition her. I hadn't thought of her, but she's an amazingly emotional actress.

LF: She has referred to *Klute* as an inspiration for her acting style, but there's also an aspect of Nicole Kidman there. Was that deliberate?

JC: They look similar, but we didn't try to make her look like Nicole. We did think of Jane Fonda in *Klute* and also of Antonioni's styling in *Blow-Up*. I looked at Coppola's *The Rain People* as well for its vérité style and at *The Godfather* for the acting style.

LF: You've combined a naturalistic acting style with rich textures in the cinematography.

JC: It's an observing camera most of the time. I did storyboard it, but tended to throw them away and find the scene as we were doing it. And we were very influenced by the locations.

LF: The film couldn't be set anywhere but New York.

JC: New York is a magnet for hopes and dreams, as well as a port where people who once had those dreams still hang around. I think of Pauline as a veteran of too many sexual adventures. She isn't dismal, though—she has problems but she's intelligent about them.

LF: The city is very eroticized in the film.

JC: Much of the eroticism comes from the locations dictated by the story. Pauline lives above a strip joint, and the one we used actually exists. We knocked on the door of the flat above it and there were students living there. The red lighthouse is clearly a phallic symbol, but with all these images I tried not to over-sweat them. What I focused on was getting the detective story working well in the hope everything else would take care of itself.

LF: The film has quite a positive ending. Do you feel there's a way through the confusion?

JC: We're always going to be caught up in contradictions and fantasies. But I think the dream of finding a soulmate is the most danger-ous—it's not that relationships don't matter, but it's dangerous to have such extraordinary hopes for them. How can a relationship complete you? That's work you have to do yourself.

LF: Where next for you?

JC: I tend just to trot ahead not knowing what'll turn up. But I actually want to take four years off to be with my daughter, who's nine now. I want to do nothing, not obligate myself to do anything.

Tissues (1980)
Australia
Director: Jane Campion
Super 8

Mishaps: Seduction and Conquest (released as *Mishaps of Seduction and Conquest*; 1981)
Australia
Production Company: Australian Film and Television School
Director: Jane Campion
Screenplay: Jane Campion
Photography: Sally Bongers, Nicolette Freeman, George Perykowski, Paul Cox
15 minutes
Cast: Emma (Deborah Kennedy), Geoffrey (Richard Evans), Mallory's Voice (Stuart Campbell)

Peel: An Exercise in Discipline (1982)
Australia
Production Company: Australian Film and Television School
Producer: Ulla Ryghe
Director: Jane Campion
Screenplay: Jane Campion
Photography: Sally Bongers
9 minutes
Cast: Tim Pye (Brother/Father), Katie Pye (Sister/Aunt), Ben Martin (Son/Nephew)

Passionless Moments (1983)
Australia
Production Company: Australian Film and Television School

Producer: Jane Campion
Director: Jane Campion
Screenplay: Jane Campion and Gerald Lee
Photography: Jane Campion
9 minutes
Cast: David Benton (Ed Tumbury), Ann Burriman (Gwen Gilbert), Sean
    Callinan (Jim Newbury), Paul Chubb (Jim Simpson), Sue Collie (Angela
    Elliot), Elias Ibrahim (Ibrahim Ibrahim), Paul Melchert (Arnold), George
    Nezovic (Gavin Metchalle), James Pride (Lyndsay Aldridge), Yves Stenning
    (Shaun), Rebecca Steweard (Julie Fry)

A Girl's Own Story (1984)
Australia
Production Company: Australian Film and Television School
Producer: Jane Campion
Director: Jane Campion
Screenplay: Jane Campion
Photography: Sally Bongers
27 minutes
Cast: Paul Chubb (Father), Jane Edwards (Dierdre), Colleen Fitzpatrick
    (Mother), Joanne Gabbe (Sister), John Godden (Graeme), Geraldine
    Haywood (Stella), Marina Knight (Gloria), Gabrielle Shornegg (Pam)

After Hours (1984)
Australia
Production Company: Women's Film Unit of Film Australia
Director: Jane Campion
Screenplay: Jane Campion
Photography: Laurie McInnes
27 minutes
Cast: Anna Maria Monticelli (Sandra Adams), Danielle Pearse (Lorraine),
    Don Reid (John Phillips)

Dancing Daze (1985)
Director: Jane Campion
Episode of television series

Two Friends (1986)
Australia
Production Company: ABC
Producer: Jan Chapman
Director: Jane Campion
Screenplay: Helen Garner

Photography: Julien Penney
Telefeature
76 minutes
Cast: Kris Bidenko (Kelly), Emma Coles (Louise), Sean Travers (Matthew),
Kris McQuade (Louise's mother)

Sweetie (1989)
Australia
Production Company: Arenafilm, Australian Film Commission, New South
Wales Film and Television Office
Producers: William MacKinnon and John Maynard
Director: Jane Campion
Screenplay: Jane Campion and Gerald Lee
Photography: Sally Bongers
Cast: Geneviève Lemon (Dawn aka Sweetie), Karen Colston (Kay), Tom
Lycos (Louis), Jon Darling (Gordon), Dorothy Barry (Flo), Michael Lake
(Bob), Andre Pataczek (Clayton), Jean Hadgraft (Mrs. Schneller), Paul
Livingston (Teddy Schneller), Louise Fox (Cheryl), Ann Merchant (Paula),
Robin Frank (Ruth Bronwyn), Morgan (Sue Sean), Callinan (Simboo),
Diana Armer (Melony), Emma Fowler (Little Sweetie), Irene Curtis
(Mandy)

An Angel at My Table (1990)
New Zealand, Australia, Great Britain
Production Company: Hibiscus Films, New Zealand Film Commission,
Television New Zealand, Australian Broadcasting Corporation, Channel
Four
Producers: Bridget Ikin, Grant Major, and John Maynard
Director: Jane Campion
Screenplay: Laura Jones
Photography: Stuart Dryburgh
157 minutes
Cast: Kerry Fox (Janet Frame), Alexia Keogh (Young Janet), Karen
Fergusson (Teenage Janet), Iris Churn (Mother), Kevin J. Wilson (Father),
Melina Bernecker (Myrtle), Timothy Bartlett (Gussy Dymock), Hamish
McFarlane (Avril Luxon), Edith Campion (Miss Lindsay), Andrew Binns
(Bruddie), Glynis Angell (Isabel), Sarah Smuts Kennedy (June), David
Letch (Patrick), William Brandt (Bernhard), Martyn Sanderson (Frank)

The Piano (1993)
Australia, France
Production Company: CiBy 2000, New South Wales Film and Television
Office, Australian Film Commission

Producers: Jan Chapman, Alain Depardieu, Mark Turnbull
Director: Jane Campion
Screenplay: Jane Campion
Photography: Stuart Dryburgh
120 minutes
Cast: Holly Hunter (Ada), Harvey Keitel (Baines), Sam Neill (Stewart), Anna
Paquin (Flora), Kerry Walker (Aunt Morag), Geneviève Lemon (Nessie),
Tungia Baker (Hira), Ian Mune (Reverend), Peter Dennett (Head
seaman), Te Whatanui Skipwith (Chief Nihe), Pete Smith (Hone), Bruce
Allpress (Blind piano tuner), Cliff Curtis (Mana), Carla Rupuha (Heni),
Mahina Tunui (Mary)

The Portrait of a Lady (1996)
Great Britain, USA
Production Company: Polygram Filmed Entertainment
Producers: Steve Golin, Monty Montgomery, Ann Wingate, Mark Turnbull,
Ute Leonhardt, Hedron Reshoeft
Director: Jane Campion
Screenplay: Laura Jones
Photography: Stuart Dryburgh
144 minutes
Cast: Nicole Kidman (Isabel Archer), John Malkovich (Gilbert Osmond),
Barbara Hershey (Madame Serena Merle), Mary-Louise Parker (Henrietta
Stackpole), Martin Donovan (Ralph Touchett), Shelley Winters (Mrs.
Touchett), Richard E. Grant (Lord Warburton) Shelley Duvall (Countess
Gemini), Christian Bale (Edward Rosier), Viggo Mortensen (Caspar
Goodwood), Valentina Cervi (Pansy Osmond), John Gielgud (Mr.
Touchett)

Holy Smoke (1999)
USA
Production Company: Miramax
Producers: Jan Chapman, Mark Turnbull, Bob Weinstein, Harvey Weinstein,
Julie Goldstein
Director: Jane Campion
Screenplay: Anna Campion and Jane Campion
Photography: Dion Beebe
114 minutes
Cast: Kate Winslet (Ruth Barron), Harvey Keitel (P. J. Waters), Pam Grier
(Carol), Julie Hamilton (Miriam Barron), Sophie Lee (Yvonne), Dan
Wyllie (Robbie), Paul Goddard (Tim), Tim Robertson (Gilbert Barron),
George Mangos (Yani), Kerry Walker (Puss), Leslie Dayman (Bill-Bill),
Samantha Murray (Prue), Austen Tayshus (Stan), Simon Anderson (Fabio),

Dhritiman Chaterji (Chidaatma Baba), Geneviève Lemon (Rahi), Robert Joseph (Miriam's taxi driver), Jane Edwards (Priya)

In the Cut (2003)
Great Britain, USA
Production Company: Pathé Productions Ltd, Screen Gems, and Red Turtle
Producers: Effie T. Brown, Francois Ivernel, Laurie Parker, and Nicole Kidman
Director: Jane Campion
Screenplay: Jane Campion and Susanna Moore
Photography: Dion Beebe
119 minutes
Cast: Meg Ryan (Frannie Avery), Mark Ruffalo (Giovanni Malloy), Jennifer Jason Leigh (Pauline), Nick Damici (Det. Rodriguez), Micheal Nuccio (Frannie's Young Father), Alison Nega (Young Father's Fiancee), Dominick Aries (Attentive Husband), Susan Gardner (Perfect Wife), Sharrieff Pugh (Cornelius Webb), Heather Litteer (Angela Sands), Daniel T. Booth (Red Turtle Bartender), Yaani King (Frannie's Student), Frank Harts (Frannie's Student), Sebastian Sozzi (Frannie's Student), Zack Wegner (Frannie's Student), Patrice O'Neal (Hector), Funda Duval (Baby Doll Bartender), Theo Kogan (Baby Doll Bartender), Sandy Vital (Baby Doll Dancer), Sharon Riggins (Baby Doll Dancer), Karen Riggins (Baby Doll Dancer), Nancy La Scala (Baby Doll Dancer), Ami Goodheart (Baby Doll Dancer), Panicker Upendran (Taxi Driver), Kendra Zimmerman (Café Waitress), Kevin Bacon (John Graham, uncredited)

Bibliography

Allen, Richard. "Female Sexuality, Creativity, and Desire in *The Piano*." *Piano Lessons: Approaches to The Piano*. Ed. Felicity Coombs and Suzanne Gemmell. London: John Libbey, 1999. 44–63.

Alley, Elizabeth. "Janet Frame/Interviewed by Elizabeth Alley." *In the Same Room: Conversations with New Zealand Writers*. Ed. Elizabeth Alley and Mark Williams. Auckland: Auckland University Press, 1992. 39–54.

Alysen, Barbara. "Australian Women in Film." *An Australian Film Reader*. Ed. Albert Moran and Tom O'Regan. Sydney: Currency Press, 1985. 302–13.

American Heritage Dictionary. Ed. William Morris. New York: American Heritage Publishing Company, 1973.

Anker, Conrad, and David Roberts. *The Lost Explorer: Finding Mallory on Mount Everest*. New York: Simon and Schuster, 1999.

Australia. Parliament. "Australian Film and Television School Annual Report." *Parliamentary Papers 1982–1983*. 8 March 1984. Number 33.

———. "Australian Film and Television School Annual Report." *Parliamentary Papers 1982–1983*. 20 Feb. 1986. Number 51.

Bauer, Dale. "Jane Campion's Symbolic *Portrait*." *The Henry James Review*. 18.2 (Spring 1997): 194–97.

Bentley, Nancy. "'Conscious Observation of a Lovely Woman:' Jane Campion's Portraits in Film." *The Henry James Review*. 18.2 (Spring 1997): 174–79.

Berger, John. *Ways of Seeing*. London and Hamondsworth: The British Broadcasting Corporation and Penguin Books, 1972.

Bihlmeyer, Jaime. "The (Un)Speakable FEMININITY in Mainstream Movies: Jane Campion's *The Piano*." *Cinema Journal*. 44.2 (Winter 2005): 68–88.

Bilborough, Miro. "The Making of *The Piano*." In Jane Campion and Jan Chapman. *The Piano*. New York: Hyperion, 1993. 135–53.

Bloustien, Geraldine. "Jane Campion: Memory, Motif and Music." *Continuum: The Australian Journal of Media & Culture*. 5.2 (1990): 1–8.

"Book of Ruth." *The Holy Bible*. American Standard Version. New York: Thomas Nelson and Sons, 1929. Chapters 1–4, pp. 297–99.

Bordwell, David. "The Art Cinema as a Mode of Film Practice." *Film Theory and Criticism: Introductory Readings.* New York: Oxford University Press, 1999. 716–24.

———. *Narration in the Fiction Film.* Madison: University of Wisconsin Press, 1985.

———, and Kristen Thomson. *Film Art: An Introduction.* 4th ed. New York: McGraw-Hill, 1993.

Branigan, Edward. *Narrative Comprehension and Film.* New York: Routledge, 1992.

"The British Hero Who Died on Everest." *British Studies Web Pages.* Accessed 8 Aug. 2004. http://elt.britcoun.org.pl/s_malor.htm.

Breashears, David, and Audrey Salkeld. *Last Climb: The Legendary Everest Expeditions of George Mallory.* Washington, DC: National Geographic Society, 1999.

Brooks, Peter. *The Melodramatic Imagination.* 1976. New Haven, Conn.: Yale University Press, 1995.

Brontë, Emily. *Wuthering Heights.* Norton Critical Ed. 3rd ed. Ed. William M. Sale Jr., and Richard J. Dunn. New York: W. W. Norton, 1990.

Brown, Wendy. *States of Injury: Power and Freedom in Late Modernity.* Princeton, N.J.: Princeton University Press, 1995.

Bruzzi, Stella. "Tempestuous Petticoats: Costume and Desire in *The Piano.*" *Screen.* 36.3 (Autumn 1995): 257–66.

Butler, Judith. *Precarious Life: The Powers of Mourning and Violence.* New York: Verso, 2004.

Caillois, Roger. *The Edge of Surrealism.* Ed. and with an Introduction by Claudine Frank. Trans. Claudine Frank and Camille Naish. Durham, N.C.: Duke University Press, 2003.

Campion, Jane, and Jan Chapman. *The Piano.* New York: Hyperion, 1993.

Chadwick, Whitney, ed. *Mirror Images: Women, Surrealism and Self-Representation.* Cambridge, Mass.: MIT Press, 1998.

———. "An Infinite Play of Empty Mirrors: Women, Surrealism, and Self-Representation." *Mirror Images: Women, Surrealism, and Self-Representation.* Ed. Whitney Chadwick. Cambridge, Mass.: MIT Press, 1998. 2–35.

Chandler, Karen Michele. "Agency and Social Constraint in Jane Campion's *The Portrait of a Lady.*" *The Henry James Review.* 18.2 (Spring 1997): 191–93.

Chatterjee, Piya. *A Time for Tea: Women, Labor and Post-Colonial Politics on an Indian Plantation.* Durham, N.C.: Duke University Press, 2001.

Cheshire, Ellen. *Jane Campion.* Harpenden, Great Britain: Pocket Essentials, 2000.

Clifford, James. "On Ethnographic Surrealism." *Comparative Studies in Society and History.* 23. 4 (Oct. 1981): 539–64.

Cook, Pam. "Approaching the Work of Dorothy Arzner." *Feminism and Film Theory.* Ed. Constance Penley. New York: Routledge, 1988. 46–56.

————. "Border Crossings: Women and Film in Context." *Women and Film: A Sight and Saound Reader.* Ed. Pam Cook and Philip Dodd. Philadelphia: Temple University Press, 1993. xii–xiv.

Coombs, Felicity, and Suzanne Gemmell. *Piano Lessons: Approaches to* The Piano. Sydney, Australia: John Libbey and Company, 1999.

Craven, Ian, ed. *Australian Cinema in the 1990s.* Portland, Oreg.: Frank Cass, 2001.

Deleuze, Gilles. *Masochism: Coldness and Cruelty.* New York: Zone Books, 1991.

Denby, David. "Creep Shows." Review of *In the Cut. The New Yorker.* 27 Oct. 2003: 112–13.

Dyson, Lynda. "The Return of the Repressed? Whiteness, Feminity, and Colonialism in *The Piano.*" *Screen* 36.3 (Summer 1995): 267–76.

Elsaesser, Thomas. "Tales of Sound and Fury." *Home Is Where the Heart Is: Studies in Melodrama and the Woman's Film.* Ed. Christine Gledhill. London: BFI, 1992. 43–69.

Evans, Patrick. *Janet Frame.* Boston: Twayne Publishers, 1977.

Fabian, Joannes. *Time and the Other.* New York: Columbia University Press, 2002.

Film Review and Cost Estimate Report (FRCE). Kagan World Media. Baseline. Hollywood.com.

Firstbrook, Peter. "Mallory as a Young Man." *History of Exploration: Lost on Everest.* Accessed 8 Aug. 2004. www.bbc.co.uk/history/exploration/everest/features/everest19.

Foster, Hal. *Compulsive Beauty.* Cambridge, Mass.: MIT Press, 1993.

Frame, Janet. *An Autobiography.* New York: George Braziller, 1989.

Freud, Sigmund. *Three Essays on the Theory of Sexuality.* Trans. and rev. James Strachey. New York: Basic Books, 1975.

Fuller, Graham. "Sex and Self-Danger." *Sight and Sound.* 13.11 (Nov. 2003): 16–19.

Gage, Carolyn. "No." *Broadsheet.* 204 (Spring 1994): 54.

Gass, William. "The High Brutality of Good Intentions." *The Portrait of a Lady: An Authoritative Text, Henry James and the Novel, Reviews and Criticism.* 2nd ed. Ed. Robert D. Bamberg. New York: W. W. Norton and Company, 1995.

George, Sandy and Rachel Turk. "Holy Smoke: Hallucination F/X." *Urban Cinefile.* 2 Oct. 2000. www.urbancinefile.com.au/print/article_view.asp?Article_ID=A2836&Section.

Gillett, Sue. "Angel from the Mirror City: Jane Campion's Janet Frame." *Senses of Cinema.* 10 (Nov. 2000). www.sensesofcinema.com.

————. "Engaging Modusa: Competing Myths and Fairy Tales in *In the Cut.*" *Senses of Cinema.* 31 (Apr.–June, 2004). www.sensesofcinema.com.

————. "Lips and Fingers: Jane Campion's *The Piano.*" *Screen.* 36.3 (Autumn 1995): 277–87.

————. "More Than Meets the Eye: The Mediation of Affects in Jane Campion's *Sweetie.*" *Senses of Cinema.* 1 (Dec. 1999). www.sensesofcinema.com.

————. "Never a Native: Deconstructing Home and Heart in *Holy Smoke.*" *Senses of Cinema.* 5 (April 2000). www.sensesofcinema.com.

Ginsberg, Carlo. *Clues, Myths, and the Historical Method.* Trans. John and Anne Tedeschi. Baltimore: Johns Hopkins University Press, 1986.

Glaessner, Verina, Pam Cook, and Sylvia Paskin. "Short Films: *A Girl's Own Story, Passionless Moments,* and *Peel.*" *Monthly Film Bulletin.* 57.678 (July 1990): 209–11.

Gledhill, Christine, ed. *Home Is Where the Heart Is: Studies in Melodrama and the Woman's Film.* London: BFI, 1992.

Gorbman, Claudia. "Music from *The Piano.*" *Jane Campion's* The Piano. Ed. Harriet Margolis. New York: Cambridge University Press, 2000. 42–58.

Gordon, Rebecca. "Portraits Perversely Framed: Jane Campion and Henry James." *Film Quarterly.* 56.2 (2003): 14–24.

Greene, Graham. *Brighton Rock.* New York: Viking Press, 1956.

Habegger, Alfred. *Henry James and the "Woman Business."* Cambridge: Cambridge University Press, 1989.

Harcourt, Peter. *A Dramatic Appearance: New Zealand Theater 1920–1970.* Wellington: Metheun Publications New Zealand, 1978.

Hardy, Ann. "The Last Patriarch." *Jane Campion's* The Piano. Ed. Harriet Margolis.New York: Cambridge University Press, 2000. 59–85.

Hawes, Tara. "Janet Frame: The Self as Other/Othering the Self." Department of English, University of Otago, New Zealand, *Deep South.* 1.1 (Feb. 1995).

Henke, Suzette. "Jane Campion Frames Janet Frame: A Portrait of the Artist as a Young New Zealand Poet." *Biography.* 23.4 (Fall 2004): 651–69.

Herrera, Hayden. *Frida: A Bibliography of Frida Kahlo.* New York: Harper and Row, 1983.

Hinson, Hal. "Sweetie." *Washington Post.* 2 March 1990. www.washingtonpost .com.

Howe, Desson. "Sweetie." *Washington Post.* 2 March 1990. www.washingtonpost .com.

Hughes, Robert. *The Shock of the New.* New York: Alfred A. Knopf, 1991.

Isherwood, Christopher. *My Guru and His Disciple.* New York: Farrar, Straus & Giroux, 1980.

Jacobs, Carol. "Playing Jane Campion's *Piano*: Politically." *MLN.* 109 (1994): 757–85.

James, Henry. *The Portrait of a Lady.* 2nd ed. New York: W. W. Norton and Company, 1995.

Jayamanne, Laleen. "Postcolonial Gothic: The Narcissistic Wound of Jane Campion's *The Piano.*" *Toward Cinema and Its Double.* Bloomington: Indiana University Press, 2001. 24–50.

Johnston, Claire. "Dorothy Arzner: Critical Strategies." *Feminism and Film Theory.* Ed. Constance Penley. New York: Routledge, 1988. 36–45.

Jones, Laura. *Portrait of a Lady: Screenplay Based on the Novel by Henry James.* New York: Penguin Books, 1996.

Kiley, David. *Getting the Bugs Out: The Rise and Comeback of Volkswagen in America.* New York: John Wiley and Sons, 2002.

King, Michael. *Wrestling With the Angel: A Life of Janet Frame.* Washington, DC: Counterpoint, 2000.

King, Noel, and Toby Miller. "Auteurism in the 1990s." *The Cinema Book,* 2nd ed. Ed. Pam Cook. London: BFI, 1999.

Kirn, Walter. "Texas Noir." *The New York Times Book Review.* 24 July 2005: 9.

Klinger, Barbara. "The Art Film, Affect, and the Female Viewer: *The Piano* Revisited." *Screen.* 47.1 (Spring 2006): 19–41.

Kozloff, Sarah. *Invisible Storytellers: Voice-Over Narration in American Fiction Film.* Berkeley: University of California Press, 1988.

Krauss, Rosalind. "Photography in the Service of Surrealism" *L'Amour Fou: Photography and Surrealism.* Washington, DC: Corcoran Gallery of Art and Abbeville Press, 1985.

————, and Jane Livingston. *L'Amour Fou: Photography and Surrealism.* Washington, DC: Corcoran Gallery of Art and Abbeville Press, 1985.

Lewis, Judith. "Wholly Jane." *L.A. Weekly.* 21–27 Jan. 2000: 36.

Margaroni, Maria. "Jane Campion's Selling of the Mother/land: Restaging the Crisis of the Postcolonial Subject." *Camera Obscura.* (Sept. 2003): 93–123.

Margolis, Harriet. "'A Strange Heritage': From Colonization to Transformation?" *Jane Campion's* The Piano. Ed. Harriet Margolis. Cambridge: Cambridge University Press, 2000. 1–41.

Mayne, Judith. *Woman at the Keyhole: Feminism and Women's Cinema.* Bloomington: Indiana University Press, 1990.

Mazzella, Anthony J. "The New Isabel." *The Portrait of a Lady.* Norton Critical Edition. Ed. Robert D. Bamberg. New York: Norton, 1995.

McHugh, Kathleen. "'Sounds that Creep Inside You': Female Narration and Voiceover in the Films of Jane Campion." *Style.* 35.2 (Summer 2001): 193–218.

Miklitsch, Bob. "Voice-over Castration: Modes of (Crypto-Male) Masculinity and (Neo-) Butch/Femme Style in *Forrest Gump, Exotica,* and *Bound.*" *Roll Over Adorno: Critical Theory and Popular Culture in the Post-Marxist Period.* Albany: State University of New York Press, 2006.

Modleski, Tania. "Axe the Piano Player." *Old Wives' Tales and Other Women's Stories.* New York: New York University Press, 1998. 31–46.

Molina, Caroline. "Muteness and Mutilation: The Aesthetics of Disability in Jane Campion's *The Piano.*" *The Body and the Physical: Discourses of Dis-

ability. Ed. David T. Mitchell and Sharon L. Snyder. Ann Arbor: University of Michigan Press, 1997. 267–82.

Moore, Susanna. *In the Cut.* New York: Plum, 1995.

Moran, Albert, and Tom O'Regan, eds. *An Australian Film Reader.* Sydney: Currency Press, 1985.

Mulvey, Laura. "Visual Pleasure and Narrative Cinema." *Screen.* 16.3 (Autumn 1975): 6–18.

———, and Peter Wollen. "Frida Kahlo and Tina Modotti." *Frida Kahlo and Tina Modotti.* London: Whitechapel Art Gallery, 1982.

Murphy, Kathleen. "Jane Campion's Shining Portrait of a Director." *Film Comment.* 32.6 (Nov.–Dec. 1996): 28–32.

Nadel, Alan. "The Search for Cinematic Identity and a Good Man: Jane Campion's Appropriation of James' Portrait." *The Henry James Review.* 18.2 (Spring 1997): 180–83.

Neill, Anna. "A Land Without a Past: Dreamtime and Nation in *The Piano.*" *Piano Lessons: Approaches to* The Piano. Ed. Felicity Coombs and Suzanne Gemmell. London: John Libbey, 1999. 136–47.

Orr, Bridget. "Birth of a Nation?: from *Utu* to *The Piano.*" *Piano Lessons: Approaches to* The Piano. Ed. Felicity Coombs and Suzanne Gemmell. London: John Libbey, 1999. 148–62.

Park, Douglas, and Dawn Dietrich. "In the Cut." *Film Quarterly.* 58.4 (2005): 39–46.

Paskin, Sylvia. *"Peel." Monthly Film Bulletin.* 57.678 (July 1990): 210–11.

Pihama, Leonie. "Ebony and Ivory: Constructions of the Maori in *The Piano.*" *Jane Campion's* The Piano. Ed. Harriet Margolis. Cambridge: Cambridge University Press, 2000. 114–34.

Polan, Dana. *Jane Campion.* London: BFI, 2001.

Press, Joy. "Campion: *Holy Smoke* was 'an Essay about Love, about Belief Systems.'" *Village Voice.* 22–28 Oct. 2003: 52.

Quinn, Anthony. "Lady Jane's Bloody Reign." Accessed 6 Jan. 2004. *London Telegraph Magazine.* Published 25 Oct. 2003. www.smh.au/articles/2003/10/24/1066631620423.html.

Quinn, Meredith, and Andrew L. Urban. *The Edge of the Known World: The Australian Film, Television, and Radio School: Impressions of the First 25 Years.* New South Wales and Sydney: Australian Film, Television, and Radio School, 1998.

Reid, Mark A. "A Few Black Keys and Maori Tattoos: Re-Reading Jane Campion's *The Piano* in Post-Negritude Time." *Quarterly Review of Film & Video.* 17.2 (June 2000): 107–16.

Robinson, Neil. "With Choices Like These, Who Needs Enemies?: *The Piano,* Women's Articulations, Melodrama, and the Woman's Film." *Piano Lessons: Approaches to* The Piano. Ed. Felicity Coombs and Suzanne Gemmell. London: John Libbey, 1999. 19–43.

Robson, Jocelyn, and Beverly Zalcock. *Girls' Own Stories: Australian and New Zealand Women's Films*. London: Scarlet Press, 1997.

Silverman, Kaja. *The Acoustic Mirror: The Female Voice in Psychoanalysis and Cinema*. Bloomington: Indiana University Press, 1988.

Simmons, Laurence. "From Landscape to Bodyscape: Images of the Land in *The Piano*." *Piano Lessons: Approaches to* The Piano. Ed. Felicity Coombs and Suzanne Gemmell. Sydney, Australia: John Libbey, 1999. 122–35.

Simpson, E. C. *A Survey of the Arts in New Zealand*. Wellington: Wellington Chamber Music Society, 1961.

Smelik, Anneke. *And the Mirror Cracked: Feminist Cinema and Film Theory*. New York: St. Martin's, 1998.

Sobchack, Vivian. "What My Fingers Knew: The Cinesthetic Subject, or Vision in the Flesh." *Carnal Thoughts: Embodiment and Moving Image Culture*. Berkeley: University of California Press, 2004. 53–84.

Spivak, Gayatri Chakravorty. *In Other Worlds: Essays in Cultural Politics*. New York: Routledge, 1988.

Stern, Lesley. "Independent Feminist Filmmaking in Australia." *An Australian Film Reader*. Ed. Albert Moran and Tom O'Regan. Sydney: Currency, 1985. 314–26.

Taubin, Amy. "The Wrong Man: Jane Campion Dives in the Psychosexual Abyss and Returns with a Fractured Fairy Tale." *Film Comment*. 39.6 (Nov./Dec. 2003): 51–52.

Taussig, Michael. *Mimesis and Alterity*. New York: Routledge, 1993.

Thompson, Kristen Moana. "The Sickness unto Death: Dislocated Gothic in a Minor Key." *Piano Lessons: Approaches to* The Piano. Ed. Felicity Coombs and Suzanne Gemmell. London: John Libbey, 1999. 64–82.

Tisdall, Caroline. *Joseph Beuys*. New York: Thames and Hudson, 1979.

Ulmer, Gregory L. *Applied Grammatology: Post(e)-Pedagogy from Jacques Derrida to Joseph Beuys*. Baltimore: Johns Hopkins University Press, 1985.

Walton, Priscilla L. "Jane and James Go to the Movies: Post-Colonial Portraits of a Lady." *The Henry James Review*. 18.2 (Spring 1997): 187–90.

Wexman, Virigina Wright. *Jane Campion Interviews*. Jackson: University Press of Mississippi, 1999.

———. "The Portrait of a Body." *The Henry James Review*. 18.2 (Spring 1997): 184–86.

"Who Needs a Husband." *Time*. 28 Aug. 2000: 50–51.

Williams, Linda. *Playing the Race Card: Melodramas of Black and White from Uncle Tom to O.J. Simpson*. Princeton, N.J.: Princeton University Press, 2001.

Williams, Linda Ruth. *The Erotic Thriller in Contemporary Cinema*. Bloomington: Indiana University Press, 2005.

Woodard, Josef. "Family Ties: *Sweetie* and *Tie Me Up, Tie Me Down*." *Santa Barbara (Calif.) Independent*. 4.184 (7 June 1990): 32.

cinematography: black-and-white, 40, 40–41, 46, 107, 136; to convey uncertainty and insecurity, 42; in *An Angel at My Table*, 68–69, 78; in *A Girl's Own Story*, 40, 46; in *Holy Smoke*, 110–11, 120–21; in *In the Cut*, 133–34, 136; objective and subjective perspectives, 70; in *Passionless Moments*, 39–40; in *The Piano*, 79; in *The Portrait of a Lady*, 101–2, 107; in *Sweetie*, 57

civil rights movement, 6

class differences: between Frame and Campion, 66; in *A Girl's Own Story*, 71; and hierarchical relationships, 86–87; and mimicry of colonial subordination, 93; in *Passionless Moments*, 39; in *The Piano*, 88; as power relationships, 87

Clifford, James, 13

Coda, 139–40

Collie, Sue, 37–38

colonialism: in *Mishaps: Seduction and Conquest*, 24; in *The Piano*, 79–80, 81, 84; and self-representation, 83

conquest: Britain and, 24; in *Mishaps: Seduction and Conquest*, 22, 24

crises, 2

cultural stereotypes, 112

Dancing Daze (Campion), 149

daughters: Campion's interest in, 126; in *In the Cut*, 126–28; and lost or absent mothers, 107; in Moore's novels, 126; in *Sweetie*, 53, 142n22

Day, Doris, 131

desire: and female agency, 51; in *Holy Smoke*, 118, 125; in *In the Cut*, 125, 132, 134, 136; and male subjectivity, 84; paradoxical characteristics, 21, 51; in *The Piano*, 93, 95, 118; in *The Portrait of a Lady*, 97, 102–3, sexual menace and, 45; shifting, 23

Diamond, Neil, 110, 112, 115

Dickinson, Emily, 81

discipline, 25–26

documentary footage, 18, 22, 27, 40, 58, 101

Donovan, Martin, 97

double meanings, 132

doubles, 11, 51; in Campion's films, 11, 51; in *A Girl's Own Story*, 65; in *In the Cut*, 125–26, 133; in *In the Cut* (Moore), 124; in *The Portrait of a Lady*, 104–6, 105–6; in *Sweetie*, 65

doubling: in *In the Cut*, 134, 138; in *Sweetie*, 142n18; women surrealists' use of, 11

Dryburgh, Stewart, 83

dysfunctional families: emotional pain in, 17; female protagonists' choices in, 2; focus of early films, 17; in *A Girl's Own Story*, 40, 43; options for women in, 2; in *Sweetie*, 62; techniques to concretize dynamics of, 43

editing: in *A Girl's Own Story*, 40; in *In the Cut*, 132; in *Passionless Moments*, 35; in *Peel: An Exercise in Discipline*, 17, 27–29; in *Sweetie*, 54

"enabling violations," 118

ethnography, 80; and Campion's imagination, 47; compared to surrealism, 13; in early films, 47; as framing tool, 85; in *A Girl's Own Story*, 40–41; and implication of spectators, 51, 57; Indian elements in *Holy Smoke*, 114; as influence in Campion's films, 12–13; and moral neutrality, 50; and the other, 87; *Peel: An Exercise in Discipline* as mock, 28; in *The Piano*, 80, 83, 85, 87; and revisioning industry cinema, 48; and revisionism of mainstream genres, 48; and surrealism, 13, 18, 41, 48–49, 52, 83, 87; in *Sweetie*, 55–56, 142; synthesized with subjective, 18

Faces in the Water (Frame), 76

family: and expressions of femininity, 11; in *Holy Smoke*, 114; model for *Peel: An Exercise in Discipline*, 147; in *Peel: An Exercise in Discipline*, 26–28, 30; permeation by violence and power, 2; surrealist critique of, 11

family conflict: in *A Girl's Own Story*, 40, 45; in *Peel: An Exercise in Discipline*, 28, 30

family dysfunction: in *A Girl's Own Story*,

masochism: in *An Angel at My Table*, 68, 71; Campion on emotional, 159–60; Campion's exploration of, 51; in *In the Cut*, 107; and mimicry, 88; in *The Portrait of a Lady*, 104, 106–7; and relation to sadism, 51, 79. *See also* sadism

mass culture, 48

McKew, Maxine, 109

melodrama: in American cinema, 85; fixed with ethnographic gaze, 83; and ideological import, 49; moral certainty in, 103; in *The Piano*, 82–85, 87; representational concerns of, 49; and social relationships, 49; and surrealism, 49

"melodramas of consciousness," 103

memory: in *A Girl's Own Story*, 49–50, 69; in *In the Cut*, 128; in *Passionless Moments*, 37, 39; in *The Piano*, 86; in *The Portrait of a Lady*, 102; in *Sweetie*, 65

men: Campion and, 158; in early films, 17–18, 47; in *Holy Smoke*, 57, 61; inadequate, 18; in *In the Cut*, 124–26, 136; as objects, 49; in *The Piano*, 49, 51; suffering of, 18, 49; vulnerability in, 49; and women, 23, 49, 127

mimesis, 23, 25, 51, 86–87

mimetic contagion. *See* mimetic infection

mimetic faculty, 88, 90

mimetic forms, 86–87

mimetic infection: in *Mishaps: Seduction and Conquest*, 134; in *The Piano*, 88, 90–91; in *The Portrait of a Lady*, 93; related to masochism/sadism, 51; in *Un Chien Andalou* (Dalí and Buñuel), 91

mimetic relations, 87–88, 93

mimetic structure, 99–100

mimicry: by Campion's ancestors, 93; of industry convention, 25; in *Mishaps: Seduction and Conquest*, 25; in *Peel: An Exercise in Discipline*, 30, 34; in *The Piano*, 85–89, 91–93; in *The Portrait of a Lady* (Campion), 99, 102, 125; in *The Portrait of a Lady* (James's novel), 99; and masochism, 88; as motivation, 50–51; and power, 88; and surrealism, 50–51; in *Sweetie*, 63; as visual motivation, 50–51

mirroring: in *Holy Smoke*, 116, 119; in *In the Cut*, 134; in *The Piano*, 83–84, 86; *The Piano* and *The Portrait of A Lady*, 95; in *The Portrait of a Lady*, 104, 107; in *Sweetie*, 63

mise-en-scène: in *Holy Smoke*, 111; influence of Beuys on, 12; in *In the Cut*, 134–35; in *Passionless Moments*, 34; in *Peel: An Exercise in Discipline*, 27; in *The Piano*, 82; and sense of melodrama, 48–49, 84–85

Mishaps: Seduction and Conquest, 19–26, **20**; analysis, 22–23; cinematic technique in, 25; colonialism in, 24; conquest in, 18, 21–22, 24; erotic impulses in, 22; female self-expression, 23; gender conventions in, 21; ironies in, 25–26; mimesis in, 21–22, 23; montage and erotics, 25–26; Mount Everest in, 24; narrative compared to piano, 23; objects of desire, **20**, 21, 25; power struggles in, 49; role-switching, 24; seduction compared to that in *The Piano*, 23; and spectators, 25; tragedy in, 25; voyeurism, 25

montage: in *Holy Smoke*, 110; in *Mishaps: Seduction and Conquest*, 21–22, 25; in *Peel: An Exercise in Discipline*, 26; in *The Portrait of a Lady*, 106; in *Sweetie*, 58, 60

Moore, Susanna, 123, 126, 158

moral neutrality: and feminist theory, 51; Frida Kahlo and, 12; in *Holy Smoke*, 118, 121; morality or lack thereof, 2; music and, 50; in *The Piano*, 12, 92; regarding power relationships, 49

Morrison, Mark, 71

Mortensen, Viggo, 97

mothers: in Campion's films, 107; Campion's interest in detached, 46–47; confused with the other, 88; and damage to daughters, 126; and daughters as doubles, 126; and daughters as rivals, 142n22; and daughters' erotic character, 107; in *A Girl's Own Story*, 46; in *Holy Smoke*, 46–47; in *In the Cut*, 128; in *The Portrait of a Lady*, 46–47, 107; in *Sweetie*, 46

Mount Everest, 19, 24
Mulvey, Laura, 83–84
music. *See* soundtrack, uses of
music industry, 112
My Brilliant Career (Armstrong), 16

narrational strategies, 48, 80
narrative: blurring objective, subjective
narrative states, 18, 40; Campion's
consistency of, 17; fabulist, 87; in
Mishaps: Seduction and Conquest, 25;
in *Mishaps: Seduction and Conquest*
compared to *The Piano,* 22; in *Peel:
An Exercise in Discipline,* 28–29; in
The Piano, 86–87; shifting focus in *The
Piano,* 23; as transformation of abstrac-
tions, 32
narrative arc, 114
nationalism, 24
New Zealand, 79–82, 109
New Zealand Players Company, 3–4
The New Zealand Theatre Company, 4
Nezovic, George, 39
Norgay, Tenzing, 24
Noyce, Phillip, 15
Nussbaum, Felicity, 140n9

"objective chance" as plot device, 55–56
"objective" film sources: in *A Girl's Own
Story,* 46; in *Mishaps: Seduction and
Conquest,* 21, 58; in *The Portrait of a
Lady,* 58; in *Sweetie,* 58
objects of desire, 21–22
oneiric elements, 11, 101, 106–7
opening credits: allusions to other films in
In the Cut, 130–31; *In the Cut,* 127
the other: in *An Angel at My Table,* 71;
being infected by, 23; in Campion's
films, 13; confusion with mother, 88;
and ethnography, 83, 87–88; in *Holy
Smoke,* 117, 119; in *The Piano* , 80, 93;
power of view from, 71
other, definitions of, 13
otherness, 57

The Pack (Beuys), **10**
pakeha New Zealanders, 4, 80–82, 92,
109, 143n37

Palme D'Or, 1, 13, 18
Paquin, Anna, 140n1
Passionless Moments, 33; absence of
dialogue in, 32–33; analysis, 35;
"Angela Eats Meat," 37–38; cinematic
representation of misunderstanding
in, 35–36; cinematic strategies in, 33;
cinematography in, 39–40; class differences in, 39; "Clear Up Sleepy Jeans,"
35–36; confounding objective and subjective in, 33; "Ed Played Front Row
in School," 37–38; "An Exciting One,"
34; "Focal Lengths," 33, 36; function
of memory in, 37; with Gerald Lee, 32;
and *A Girl's Own Story,* 40; "Ibrahim
Makes Sense of It," 33; image track,
34; masculinity, damaged in, 40; memory in, 37, 39; multiple temporarilities,
36; "A Neighborly Misunderstanding,"
35; "No Woodpeckers in Australia,"
34; relations between past and present,
37–38; "Scotties, Part of the Grand
Design of the Universe," 39–40; and
spectators, 35, 37–38; "What His
Mother Said," 37–39
Peel: An Exercise in Discipline, 26–32,
27, 31; analysis, 29–31; authority in,
29; editing, 29; ethnographic elements
in, 28, 32; as exercise in discipline, 27,
32; family conflicts, 28–29, 30; kinship relationships, 26, 28, 30; kinship
triangle, 30; and *Mishaps: Seduction
and Conquest,* 27; montage, 26–27;
narrative focus, 28; paradoxical characteristics, 31; parody of industry films
in, 27; relationship between words and
moving images, 31; screen direction,
29; sound, uses of, 30; and spectators,
27; synopsis, 26; as "true story," 27–28;
violence in, 30; voyeurism in, 27; wom-
en's bodies in, 29
perceptions of self, 11
The Piano, 78–93, **90;** awards, 140n1;
Bluebeard production in, 82, 86, 91–
92; body parts in, 85; Campion's autoethnographic impulse in, 80; colonialism, 81, 84, 93; confounding objective
and subjective in, 33; digits as motif in,

triangles: erotic, in *A Girl's Own Story,*
40; in *Peel: An Exercise in Discipline,*
27; in *Sweetie,* 64; postcolonial in *Holy
Smoke,* 113

Victoria University (Wellington), 5
violation: in Campion's films, 11, 139;
enabling, 118; in *Holy Smoke,* 116; in
The Piano, 118
violence: colonialism, patriarchy as modes
of, 87–88; in early films, 17–18; as
enabling resistance, 118; in *Peel: An
Exercise in Discipline,* 30; and unequal
access to power, 93; women's encounters with, 51
visual puns, 52, 54, 66, 79, 93, 102
voiceover narration: in *An Angel at
My Table,* 67, 69, 75–76, 77; in *Holy
Smoke,* 110, 115, 120, 122, 125; in *In
the Cut,* 135; in *Mishaps: Seduction
and Conquest,* 18, 25; in narrative
strategy, 48; in *Passionless Moments,*
32, 34–35, 35–36, 37–38, 39, 39–40; in
The Piano, 79, 85; in *The Portrait of
a Lady,* 94, 125; in *Sweetie,* 53–54; in
tension with other narrative structures,
52
voyeurism: erotic, 27; in *In the Cut,* 134;
in *Mishaps: Seduction and Conquest,*
25; in *The Piano,* 88–89; realist, 27

Walker, Kerry, 84
Williams, Linda, 48
Wilson, Kevin J., 69
women: bad choices by, 51, 104, 125,
136; characteristics of, 18; choices in
dysfunctional families, 2; contemporary
antipodean, 95, 109; creative expression and, 18; and desire, 51; emancipation of white European, 25; in the "finger trilogy," 109; in *A Girl's Own Story,*
40–41; importance of their work, 18; in
industry cinema, 25; as objects of the
gaze, 25; patriarchal oppression of, 80;
perverse character of choice for, 103;
qualities in Campion films, 18; in relation to colonialism, 79; relationships
among, 114; and romantic love, 95; and
sexuality, 107–8; and sexual desire, 18;
vulnerability in, 49
women filmmakers: arts training and, 16;
and Australian Film Television and
Radio School (AFTRS), 14, 16, 140n6;
in film industry history, 16
women's bodies, 2, 11
Women's Film Fund, 16
women's relationships, 114
women surrealists, 11

Yarborough, Richard, 140n9

Kathleen McHugh is a professor of English and film, television, and digital media at the University of California, Los Angeles. She is the author of *American Domesticity: From How-To Manual to Hollywood Melodrama*, the coeditor of *South Korean Golden Age Melodrama: Gender, Genre and National Cinema*, and the coeditor of a special issue of *SIGNS* on Film Feminisms.

Books in the series *Contemporary Film Directors*

The University of Illinois Press
is a founding member of the
Association of American University Presses.

———————————————————————

Composed in 10/13 New Caledonia
with Helvetica Neue display
by Jim Proefrock
at the University of Illinois Press
Designed by Paula Newcomb
Manufactured by Sheridan Books, Inc.

University of Illinois Press
1325 South Oak Street
Champaign, IL 61820-6903
www.press.uillinois.edu